APPEARANCES AND MIRACLES

OF THE VIRGIN MARY

APPEARANCES AND MIRACLES

of the Virgin Mary

Compiled by
Holy Monastery of the Paraclete
Oropos, Attica, Greece

Uncut Mountain Press

APPEARANCES AND MIRACLES OF THE VIRGIN MARY

Uncut Mountain Press
Florence, AZ
uncutmountainpress.com

+1 (520) 895-1804 | info@uncutmountainpress.com

Scriptural quotations are taken from the KJV. For the Old Testament, where the KJV differs from the Greek, quotations are from Sir Lancelot Brenton's translation of the Septuagint. Quotations from the Psalms are taken from *The Psalter According to the Seventy* by Holy Transfiguration Monastery in Brookline, MA. Quotations from the liturgical texts of the Church are likewise taken from the translations of Holy Transfiguration Monastery.

Images are from Uncut Mountain Supply or in the public domain unless cited otherwise.

The first English translation and publication of this collection of texts was undertaken by Fr. Ermolaos Iatrou from the thirty-ninth edition of the Holy Monastery of the Paraclete, Oropos, Attica, in Greece. This second English edition presents a text thoroughly edited and revised by Uncut Mountain Press.

Appearances and Miracles of the Virgin Mary—2nd English ed.
Compiled by the Holy Monastery of the Paraclete.
Translated and edited by Uncut Mountain Press.

ISBN (softcover): 978-1-63941-084-2
ISBN (ebook): 978-1-63941-085-9

I. Eastern Orthodox Church
II. Eastern Orthodox Spirituality

Printed in Canada.

"There is nothing in life like the Theotokos Mary. Traverse, O man, all creation with your thought and see if there is anything equal to or greater than the holy Theotokos Virgin. Roam the earth, survey the sea, investigate the air, search the heavens with your mind, consider all the invisible Powers, and see if there is another such wonder in all creation."

— St. John Chrysostom
(as quoted in the Prologue)

CONTENTS

Father Ermolaos Iatrou

PUBLISHER'S NOTE

The publication of this book is largely due to the work and encouragement of a dear friend and outstanding modern Orthodox missionary to Africa, the ever-memorable Fr. Ermolaos Iatrou. Father Ermolaos worked absolutely tirelessly to bring the Gospel and the Faith to the far reaches of the African continent, including arranging for the first translation and edition of this book, which he asked us to perfect and publish for English speakers in North America.

Father Ermolaos was exceptional in many ways, not least of all as one of a very few married clergymen who has his family in the missionary field. He was largely responsible for the establishment and tremendous growth of the Orthodox Church in Malawi, where he built the Church of Saint Nektarios, and many other churches, with the help of many young men whom he had catechized and guided to the priesthood. He was their father, their inspiration, and he nurtured a generation of African clergymen who now serve the Orthodox Church with zeal.

Father Ermolaos was a rare clergyman for another reason. He strove to follow with exactitude the Holy Fathers, eschewing every innovation and heresy of our day with great boldness. His principled stand on matters of Faith led him to other missionary outposts. Having overcome grave illness during the time of the so-called pandemic, he continued his mission undeterred, moving to the yet-to-be touched missionary field of Liberia, to extend the Light of Orthodoxy to new souls.

It was there, in the midst of his holy work, that the Lord called him suddenly to the heavenly realm on the first of April 2022. All who knew him mourned his loss even as they remember his zeal and love for the Incarnate Truth with gratitude and reverence. He offered not only his last bit of strength for the Gospel but also his learning, generously entrusting to us translations of spiritual classics such as this, that the treasures of the Faith might enrich many others.

May the sacrifice, love, zeal and missionary spirit of the ever-memorable Fr. Ermolaos continue to inspire all who encounter his work and the fruit of his labors. Memory Eternal, dear Father Ermolaos!

Father Ermolaos Iatrou

Praise of the Mother of God (17th century icon), Crete

PROLOGUE

Mary the Theotokos, first among the saints, was the person "foretold by the Prophets" and "chosen from all generations" to cooperate in the mystery of the Incarnation of God the Word.

The name Mary, which was given to the Theotokos "according to the foreknowledge and will of God," is interpreted as "Lady." Saint Nicodemus gives the name a triple interpretation: lady, illumination, and sea, which denote respectively the power, wisdom, and goodness of the Theotokos. From the Father, she received power, so that as a Mother on earth she might fulfill what God fulfills as a Father in heaven. From the Son, she received wisdom as His Mother, so that she might be able to reconcile God with man. From the Holy Spirit, finally, she received goodness as His Bride so that she might transmit spiritual gifts to all creation.

From her very birth, the holy life of the Theotokos is interwoven with wondrous events and filled with exceptional blessings. She alone, of all women, was born of a promise—that is, after an angelic prophecy.

After three years, she was led by divine guidance to the Holy of Holies "as a three-year-old heifer," where, according to John of Damascus, "planted and fattened by the Spirit like a fruitful olive tree, she became the dwelling place of every virtue." There the Theotokos Mary remained for twelve years and was supernaturally nourished with heavenly food. God was thus preparing her for the great ministry of the incarnate economy. He was preparing her to make her "full of grace"—that is, to adorn her with all the gifts of the Holy Spirit.

When the fullness of time had come, an angel of the Lord is sent to the Virgin and announces to her the conception of the Son of God. She humbly and obediently accepted the highest honor and, "full of the Holy Spirit," exclaimed, "My soul magnifies the Lord, and my spirit has rejoiced in God my Savior, for He has regarded the lowliness of His handmaiden."

With no other virtue did the Theotokos draw God's condescension as much as with humility. He who humbled Himself to the point of death on a cross indeed needed such a humble mother.

This unprecedented humility, according to Saint Nicodemus, was not only rooted in the depths of her heart, but from there it welled up and flooded her all-blameless body, her movements, her attire, her works, and her words.

The utmost humility of the Theotokos is rivaled by her purity. Saint Gregory Palamas states that the Panagia surpassed even the angels in purity.

Many of the Fathers also agree that the Theotokos was entirely a stranger to sin. The verse from the Song of Songs, "Thou art all fair, my love; there is no spot in thee," perfectly fits and characterizes the purity of the Virgin.

At the Annunciation, the Theotokos was freed, by the descent of the Holy Spirit, even from that common defilement of humanity, the ancestral sin. Thus, she was deemed worthy to become a divine dwelling place and to minister in the supernatural mystery of the Incarnation of God the Word. This mystery was accomplished without corrupting the purity of the Virgin because the Theotokos conceived, carried, and bore the Lord without seed and without corruption. Thus, she was preserved a virgin before, during, and after the birth of the Lord, and remained Ever-Virgin.

The entire life of the Panagia was a continuous divine doxology. But also her blessed dormition was a worthy seal of her life.

Three days after her burial by the holy apostles, she "was translated to life"—that is, her God-receiving body was transferred to heaven, where her holy soul had preceded it, and where she now enjoys the eschatological incorruption of eternity.

Saint Mark of Ephesus melodiously summarizes this remarkable event: "The Mother of Life accepts death and, having been placed in a tomb, after the third day is gloriously raised up to reign with her Son for ages and to ask for the forgiveness of our trespasses."

The golden-mouthed saint [John Chrysostom], astonished by the majesty of the Theotokos, challenges the faithful to search and find a similar wondrous being: "There is nothing in life like the Theotokos Mary. Traverse, O man, all creation with your thought and see if there is anything equal to or greater than the holy Theotokos Virgin. Roam the earth, survey the sea, investigate the air, search the heavens with your mind, consider all the invisible Powers, and see if there is another such wonder in all creation."

After her divine translation, the Theotokos co-reigns with her Son in the heavens. From this honored position, she dynamically supports humanity. She has the "power to will that is equal in balance," because she lent her flesh "to the all-skillful Word," Who for this reason is eternally her debtor, according to Saint Nicodemus. Possessing such power, the Theotokos "conveys" divine gifts to all, intercedes with her saving intercessions on behalf of mankind, and influences the counsels of her Son.

Her miraculous grace, distinct and more powerful than that of the other saints, is manifested to people in many ways. Thus, the Panagia appears as a champion leader in wars, an unmercenary physician in illnesses, and a "swift protection and help" in every need.

* * *

The gratitude, trust, and love of the faithful people for the Panagia are imprinted in hymnography, folklore, art, and worship. Many churches and monasteries are dedicated to the Theotokos. In her honor, a multitude of holy icons have been artfully made. But also hymns, troparia, services, and feasts have their reference to the Mother of God. Many holy pilgrimage sites are established in areas associated with the miracles of the Panagia. In traditions, beliefs, and popular proverbs, the name of the Theotokos is mentioned with exceptional honor and reverence.

Besides the basic feasts of the Theotokos, the life of the church and popular piety have added many others, which are related to wondrous acts of the Mother of God, to the consecrations of her churches, or to the findings of her miraculous icons. In Russia, the feasts of the Panagia held in honor of her miraculous icons amount to two hundred.

The many votive offerings with which Theotokos icons are laden constitute another proof of popular gratitude towards her. Every place has a miraculous icon of the Panagia, each with its own history and legends, which create an atmosphere of religious mystery.

Of the ecclesiastical services that refer to the Panagia, the most popular are the Salutations of Great Lent and the

Paraklesis (Supplicatory Canon) services of the Dormition Fast.

Many epithets have been given to the Theotokos, expressive and sometimes paradoxical adjectives, which correspond to her qualities, to her iconographic types, to the time of her feasts, etc. Such names include: Odigitria (She Who Shows the Way), Glykophilousa (Sweet-Kissing), Gorgoepikoos (Quick to Hear), Portaitissa (Keeper of the Gate), Prousiotissa (of Proussa), Phaneromeni (The Revealed), Zoodochos Pigi (Life-Giving Spring), Myrtidiotissa (of the Myrtle Tree), etc.

Zoodochos Pigi (Life-Giving Spring), 17th century icon

* * *

The miracles of the Panagia which—only as a sample—we have included in this book come from various sources. We offer them adapted and enriched with the necessary geographical and historical information, without, however, altering their essence at all.

The number noted at the end of each text, within brackets, refers to the main source related to the subject, which is found numbered and in alphabetical order by author at the end of the book.

In these miracles, the Theotokos comes into direct contact with people and their problems. Often she appears [to people] during sleep or in a waking state. Other times,

Panagia Odigitria

her presence is made perceptible only by her voice or by some fragrance.

In all these ways, she intervenes miraculously and heals illnesses, encourages warriors, satisfies needs, saves from dangers, and gives solutions to problems and impasses. Other times she guides people to the finding of her holy icons, and other times she evangelizes benefactions or, conversely, foretells misfortunes. Similarly, she stigmatizes disorder and irreverence or rewards virtue. Finally, she leads to repentance, converts those of other faiths, and exemplarily punishes blasphemers.

However, for this living presence of the Theotokos in both the individual and the common life of Christians to be perceived and accepted, it presupposes an equally living faith. This truth is characteristically emphasized by a Matins Theotokion of January 10:

"Let faith alone lead, and not proof of the miracles beyond understanding, O God-bearing maiden; for you bore the incomprehensible God the Word, Who put on humanity...."

Panagia Glykophilousa (The Sweetly-Kissing),
Philotheou Monastery, Mount Athos, Greece

PART I

MIRACULOUS ICONS

Panagia Portaitissa (Keeper of the Gate)
Iviron Monastery, Mount Athos, Greece

Panagia Portaitissa (Keeper of the Gate)

The miraculous Portaitissa, the most prominent among the icons of the Theotokos of Athos, was originally kept, as tradition recounts, in Nicaea of Asia Minor. A pious woman and her only son, a monk, had placed it in their private church and honored it.

During the second period of Iconoclasm, royal spies discovered the icon and threatened the woman, stating that they would kill her if she did not pay them. She promised she would give them the money the next day. That night, after praying before the icon, she lifted it with reverence, went down to the shore, and cast it into the sea, saying:

"Lady Theotokos, you have the power both to save us from the king's wrath and your icon from sinking."

Then, truly, something wondrous happened. The miraculous icon stood upright on the waves and headed west. Moved by this event, the woman turned to her son and said, "My child, for the love of the Panagia, I am ready to die. You must leave. Go to Greece."

Without delay, her son prepared and set off for Thessaloniki, and from there to Athos, where he became a monk. As a monk, he practiced asceticism in the place where the Iviron Monastery was later founded. This was by God's providence, for it was thus that the other monks learned the history of the miraculous icon.

Time passed. The monk from Nicaea died, and the Iviron Monastery was founded and completed. One evening, the monks beheld a strange sight: a pillar of fire starting from the sea and reaching the sky. The vision lasted days and nights. The brothers went down to the shore and saw, with wonder, an icon of the Theotokos at the base of the pillar of fire. However, the closer they approached, the further it moved away. They then gathered in the church and tearfully begged the Lord to grant this priceless treasure to their monastery.

Among the monks was a pious ascetic named Gabriel. The Panagia appeared to him and said, "Tell the abbot and the brothers that I will give you my icon to protect you. You will then enter the sea, walk upon the waves, and thus everyone will understand my favor towards your monastery."

And so it happened. Father Gabriel walked upon the sea as if on dry land, received the miraculous icon with reverence, and returned to the shore. There, all the monks gathered and accorded it an honorable welcome. Afterward, they took it and placed it in the sanctuary of the main church (katholikon).

The next day, when the ecclesiarch went to light the oil lamps, the icon was missing. He searched everywhere and discovered it on the wall, above the monastery gate. They brought it back to the katholikon, but the icon left again. This happened many times. Finally, the Panagia appeared to the elder Gabriel and told him, "Tell the brothers not to disturb me. I did not come here to be guarded by you, but to guard you. As long as you live virtuously on this Mountain, hope in the mercy of my Son. For as long as my icon exists within your monastery, His grace and mercy will always overshadow you."

After this, the monks built a chapel near the gate and placed the holy icon there. Indeed, the Portaitissa protects the monastery and provides for its every need, as she promised.

Panagia Portaitissa

The Healing of the Princess

In 1651, the 365 monks of Iviron were experiencing financial hardship, so they entreated the Theotokos to provide for their sustenance. Immediately, the loving Mother hastened to find resources through the following grace-filled miracle.

During that period, the daughter of the Tsar of Russia Alexei Mikhailovich was gravely ill. Her legs were paralyzed and, according to the doctors, incurable. The sorrow of the princess and her royal parents was now to be turned into joy by the miraculous Portaitissa. One night, she appeared to the princess in her sleep, and after encouraging her and promising to heal her, she said, "Tell your father to bring my icon, the Portaitissa, from the Monastery of Iviron."

In the morning, the sick girl relayed the command, and immediately a special mission set out to convey the Tsar's wish to the monks of Iviron. The monks feared that the icon might not be returned and decided to send a faithful copy with an honor guard of four hieromonks.

As soon as the venerable icon's arrival in Moscow became known, the city emptied. Everyone, royals and common folk alike, ran to welcome it. However, in the palace, the princess lay in bed, unaware of anything. At some point, she asked for her mother and was then informed of the great event.

"What?" she cried. "The Panagia is coming and they left me here?"

She immediately jumped out of bed, dressed, and ran to welcome the Panagia herself. The crowd saw the paralyzed princess running and was astonished. The emotion peaked when, from the other side, the holy icon arrived, and the ceremony of welcome and veneration took place.

"Your Majesty," said the envoys, "we offer this venerable icon as a gift to the pious Russian nation."

"Thank you," said the Tsar, deeply moved. "As a token of my gratitude, I grant you one of the best monasteries in the capital, Saint Nicholas. Also, an annual stipend of 2,500 rubles, tax exemption on whatever you import and export from my country, as well as free travel for your envoys."

This metochion (monastery dependency) remained under the ownership of the Iviron Monastery until 1932 and secured so much income for it that it covered almost all its material needs.

The Hungry Wayfarer

The Monastery of Iviron is a very hospitable monastery. This is also attributed to the following incident.

A poor worker, tired from the road, arrived hungry at the monastery gate at noon. He asked the gatekeeper only for a little bread because he was in a hurry to continue his journey. The gatekeeper, for unknown reasons, did not give him any, so the poor man sighed deeply and left hungry.

Ascending towards Karyes, he stopped for a while in the shade of a tree. Sad and tired as he was, he lay on the ground. Suddenly, he heard footsteps approaching. He sat up and saw near him a woman with an infant in her arms.

With a sympathetic expression and a sweet voice, she asked him, “What is wrong? Are you perhaps ill?”

“No,” he replied, “but I am hungry. I asked the gatekeeper of the Iviron Monastery to give me bread, but he didn’t.”

“Listen, my child. You should not complain about the gatekeeper. I am the gatekeeper of this monastery. Return immediately and ask for bread in my name. And if they do not give it to you, pay for it with this money. I will wait for you here.”

Upon saying this, she gave the worker three gold coins (florins). Unsuspecting of what he had seen and heard, the worker set off for the monastery. He knocked on the gate and, ostentatiously holding the money, asked the gatekeeper again for bread, not failing to mention his conversation with the woman.

When the monk heard about the woman and saw the rare coins, he realized it was a miracle. He rang the bell, the brothers gathered, and listened with amazement to the extraordinary event. They even determined that those coins had been dedicated many years ago to the miraculous icon. However, the Panagia, seeing the poor man’s need, had taken them and given them to him with motherly compassion.

The monks, with fear and reverence, returned them to the holy icon of the Portaitissa, who, through this miracle, taught them the great virtue of hospitality.

[41]

Panagia Paramythia (Consolation)

In January of the year 807, the Algerian pirate Vardoukhan, using Milos as his base of operations, plundered the Aegean islands and the coasts of Thrace and Asia Minor with his seventeen pirate ships.

Panagia Paramythia (8th century)
Monastery of Vatopedi, Mount Athos, Greece

In this month, he decided to turn against Mount Athos. He prepared ten ships, took two hundred pirates with him, and set out for the Monastery of Vatopedi.

Panagia Paramythia

At dawn on January 21, they anchored in the monastery's small harbor, came ashore, and waited in hiding for the morning opening of the gate so they could storm in.

The monks had just finished the Matins service and were retiring to their cells to rest. Only the abbot remained in the church, continuing his prayer. Suddenly, he heard a voice from the icon of the Panagia, saying, "Do not open the gates today. Go up to the walls and drive away the pirates."

Astonished by the strange sound, he turned and looked at the Theotokos. Then he saw another more astounding miracle: the faces of the Panagia and the Divine Infant had come alive. At the same moment, the young Jesus stretched out His hand, covered the mouth of His Mother, the Panagia, and turning His face towards her, said, "No, mother, do not say it! Let them be punished as they deserve!"

But the Panagia took her Son's hand, turned her face slightly to the right, and said again, "Do not open the gates of the monastery today!"

The abbot, deeply moved, gathered the monks and recounted the wondrous things he had seen and heard. And they observed with awe that the holy faces on the icon of the Theotokos had changed posture and expression. Afterward, having thanked the Panagia for her saving providence, they ascended the walls.

The time had come: the pirates, with ladders and axes, were preparing to climb. The abbot, standing on the battlements, first let them approach. Then, raising the Holy Cross, he gave the signal for repulsion. Ten pirates immediately fell dead, others were wounded, and the rest got into their ships and fled.

The monks descended to the church and thanked the Theotokos once more. Since then, the icon took the name "Paramythia," meaning consolation, and remains changed to this day to commemorate that wondrous event.

[39]

Panagia Eikosifoinissa (of the Twenty Palm Trees)

The Monastery of Panagia Eikosifoinissa, with its miraculous icon not made by hands [*acheiropoieton*], dominates the lush green landscape, perched on the slopes of Mount Pangaion. The Theotokos herself, through an angel, instructed the first founder, Saint Germanos (ninth century), to erect the monastery. And since then, she has not ceased, in every manner, to care for and take interest in it.

One day, she appeared to an eighteen-year-old youth who was plowing near the monastery and said to him, "Come, I need you. I have need in my monastery." Like another Elisha, he left the animals yoked and immediately set off for the monastery, where he became a monk with the name Damaskinos (Tsombaxis), and later the abbot. Father Damaskinos would see the Panagia inside the church, overseeing things. And when he ascended the stairs to the cells, he would see her descending, and vice versa.

One night in 1908, Turkish bandits approached the monastery. The gate was secured with heavy iron bars, so they left one guard there while the others hammered nails to climb the wall. Suddenly, they heard the guard shouting, "Help, save me! A woman dressed in black has grabbed me by the hair. Help!" The terrified Turks immediately jumped down from the wall and fled.

Panagia Eikosifoinissa
Monastery of Panagia Eikosifinissa,
Mount Pangaion, Greece

The Raid of the Bulgarians

After a turbulent historical course for the monastery marked by glory, radiance, offerings, but also calamities, it entered the period of the first Bulgarian occupation in 1916-1918, when it suffered criminal attacks by the Bulgarians. Their goal was to steal the miraculous acheiropoieton icon of the Theotokos.

One of the many unsuccessful attempts occurred on June 23, 1917. The monks were at Vespers and had brought out the holy relics for veneration. At that moment, the Bulgarians entered the church. The fathers tried to hide the relics, but the Bulgarians protested. "Don't take them," they said. "Leave them for us to venerate. We are Christians too."

However, this was a deceitful trick because they immediately snatched the holy relics and fled. The next day, they set their sights on taking the miraculous icon. A sergeant, along with others, tried to lift it, but he fell dead, and his pistol and boot were indelibly imprinted on the marble floor of the church.

In another attempt, the Bulgarians managed to remove the icon from its place, but as soon as they reached the church door, the icon fell down. It became so heavy that not even a crane could lift it. At the same time, the Panagia wept loudly, and her tears formed a small stream on the holy icon. The sacrilegious men were confused. They abandoned their attempt and fled in terror.

Abandonment of the Monastery

During the period of the guerrilla war, in the second Bulgarian occupation, the monks were notified one day to abandon the monastery because their lives were in danger. Villagers from the area immediately rushed with two hundred animals to take whatever they could from the monastery and hide it in their homes. Then something wondrous happened: the icons came out of their places on their own, and the faithful received them. And when they came out of the church, they saw all the monastery animals (chickens, dogs, and pigs) lined up outside the narthex, crying out. Thousands of birds were also chirping on the domes of the church. Thus, they, too, participated in the general sorrow for the departure of the Lady of the Angels, whose icon pious men carried in their hands. And when the caravan set off for the village of Nikisiani, the monastery animals also followed sadly. They did not want to be left behind alone. But even when the monastery remained deserted, a shepherd from the area, Nikos Katsikaris, would hear the bells, the semantron, and the talanton ringing joyfully on the nights of Christmas, Pascha, and the feasts of the Theotokos. What did it matter if humans were absent? Angels served at Eikosifoinissa.

[14]

Panagia of Lithines

Panagia of Lithines (14th century)
Holy Church of Panagia of Lithina,
Sitia, Greece

In Crete, in the village of Lithines in the province of Siteia, there is an ancient church of the Panagia, which celebrates its feast day on September 8. On its iconostasis, the icon of the Panagia of Lithines stands out, framed with countless votive offerings, for it is very miraculous. The church has a large courtyard and a guesthouse. Often, the inhabitants pass through the church courtyard to take a shortcut and reach their homes faster. However, if they buy meat and pass through there during a fasting period (such as Great Lent), the meat develops worms, which are easily visible.

This miracle did not only happen in older times. Some modern skeptics conducted an experiment. They bought fresh meat during a fasting period and passed through the church courtyard. They, too, confirmed that the meat had become infested with worms. Once, a butcher tried to pass through holding half a lamb. However, midway through the courtyard, his legs became paralyzed, and he fell down shouting in terror.

In this way, the Theotokos reinforces the institution of fasting in the conscience of the faithful.

[12]

Panagia Neamonitissa

Fragrant Chios, called "rugged" by Homer due to its rocky and mountainous terrain, was considered by the ancients one of the "Blessed Isles" for its natural advantages. This name would suit it metaphorically also for the piety of its inhabitants. In antiquity, it was full of statues and pagan temples. But even in the Christian era, the multitude of its sacred churches intrigues every visitor. "Chian society," noted M. Justinian in 1606, "is most devout, while its clergy is much more remarkable than that of other regions." It also has many saints and monasteries.

A few kilometers from the island's capital, at the foot of Mount Provatas, stands the most notable monastery of Chios, the ancient Nea Moni. This patriarchal stavropegic monastery, with its imperial golden bulls and famous mosaics, is fortified by natural and artificial walls and towers, parts of which survive to this day. The construction work of the monastery began in 1034 by the Chian ascetics Nikitas, Joseph, and John. A valuable supporter in their effort was the Byzantine emperor Constantine IX Monomachos.

In the tradition of the monastery's history, the miraculous finding of the Panagia Neamonitissa is widespread. The three founders discovered this miraculous icon in a dense forest, surrounded by impenetrable brambles and

Panagia Neamonitissa,
Monastery of Nea Moni, Chios, Greece

undergrowth. The divine form of the Theotokos is depicted in a peculiar and unique stance: she holds the Divine Infant in her hands and is shown standing, with her maternal embrace open and her feet in a walking posture. The sacred icon of Neamonitissa is often miraculously saved from fires itself, and also saved Nea Moni from massacres, raids, and other adversities it experienced throughout its history.

The Goldsmith

Once, the monks commissioned a Chian goldsmith to cover a part of the sacred icon with gold to protect it from decay. The ecclesiarch placed it in the main church, and the artisan began his work with reverence. Suddenly, he heard a sweet voice whisper to him, "Tap lightly, lightly; may you have my blessing, because the icon is old!"

The goldsmith lifted his eyes and saw a majestic woman in fully gold attire. He didn't have time to ask who she was, because she immediately entered the sanctuary through the south gate. He ran to catch her, but she had disappeared. He entered the sanctuary, and then recognized in the form of the Platytera the woman who had appeared to him moments before.

The Bell

The bell tower of Nea Moni resembles a square tower and rises almost three stories high, reaching up to the dome of the katholikon. It is roofed with lead and adorned at the top with a beautiful iron cross. Originally, it had four bells and two very ornate clocks. However, everything disappeared in 1822 at the hands of the Asiatic hordes.

Once, one of the largest bells cracked. The monks loaded it onto a Venetian ship and sent it to Venice to be recast. While sailing, the ship was attacked by a corsair ship of Barbarossa's pirates and was in danger of sinking. The sailors, in that difficult moment, invoked the help of Panagia Neamonitissa. Then they broke off a piece of the bell, used it as a cannonball, loaded it into the cannon, and struck the enemy ship. The hit was critical, and the pirate ship sank.

The Venetian ship continued its journey and reached its destination. The captain, out of gratitude for their salvation, had the bell repaired at his own expense and offered it as a gift to the Panagia. It is even said that this bell was the most melodic of all.

The Wood and the Rope

A Chian ship, while sailing, encountered a great storm. The captain, facing danger, cried out with his fervent island faith, "My Panagia Neamonitissa, save us! And I vow to you a candle as tall as the ship's mast!"

He had barely finished his words when he saw on the foamy sea the Theotokos herself, holding a piece of wood and a rope in her hand. Then she sank into the waves.

Immediately the storm subsided, and the ship anchored safely in the harbor. There, to their great surprise, they discovered a hole in its hull. This hole was plugged with a piece of wood and a piece of rope.

The miracle of the Panagia was evident. Immediately, the entire crew, full of gratitude, set off for Nea Moni. They venerated the miraculous icon, offered their vow, a huge candle, and left the saving wood and rope in the exonarthex, where they remain to this day. For the same reason, it is said, there is also a sponge in the exonarthex. By the grace of Neamonitissa, this sponge plugged the crack of a sailing ship that was in danger of sinking.

The Mule

In the seventeenth century, as foreign travelers note, Nea Moni numbered one hundred to one hundred fifty monks and resembled a small city. The number of pack animals for transporting the many revenues was correspondingly large. Once, a pilgrim from Mytilene handed over a load of oil for the monastery to the *vourdonaris* [muleteer supervisor] of Nea Moni's animals. The vourdonaris loaded the mule and set off.

When they reached the chapel of Saint Phanourios, which was in a rough spot, the animal stumbled and fell down the precipice to the river. The vourdonaris, certain the mule was killed, didn't bother further with it. However, he recounted the sad episode to the monks. Not much time passed before knocks and neighs were heard at the monastery gate. The gatekeeper ran to open it and saw the mule that had fallen. The most wondrous thing was that it still had the skins of oil loaded safely on its back. The gatekeeper brought it inside and unloaded it. But then the following paradox occurred: the animal immediately fell to the ground dead. It had fulfilled its mission.

The Pious Donor

A pious Chian woman from the village of Kalimassia dedicated her entire fortune to Nea Moni. However, she once fell ill and found herself in great financial need. Then her relatives, instead of helping her, abandoned her and embittered her with harsh words. "Let Nea Moni come and look after you," they told her, "since you wrote your property over to it."

She did not cease to pray fervently to the Panagia, asking for her help. And one evening, amidst her pain and despair, she saw a woman in her sleep. This woman approached her, comforted her, and among other things, told her, "Do not be afraid. Your illness has been cured. Take this gold coin (florin), and I will take care of you."

"Who are you?" asked the sick woman.

"I am Nea Moni."

With these words, the woman awoke cured, holding the florin in her right hand. She went to the monastery, recounted her dream to the abbot, Anthimos, and handed him the florin that the Panagia had gifted her.

Wondrous Events

When the monastery was converted into a convent, the nuns experienced certain wondrous events.

At midnight on April 4, 1959, the bells rang joyfully. They rang on their own, while simultaneously a blinding light emanated from the church.

Several times, the oil lamps in front of the miraculous icon moved on their own, and often, while the nuns are chanting at the *analogion* (lectern), footsteps are heard in the sanctuary, and also loud noises, and exceedingly sweet psalmody. These chants, as the sisters affirm, are mainly heard when the Ninth Ode, the "Axion Estin [It is Truly Meet]," and the Salutations to the Theotokos are chanted.

With these wondrous signs, the Neamonitissa makes her presence felt in the monastery and imparts joy and consolation to the monastic sisterhood.

[5]

Panagia Cassiopia

Around the year 1530, in Venetian-occupied Corfu, an honest young man named Stephen was returning one day from the city to his village. On the road, he met other travelers, and so they all walked together in company. At some point, they discerned in the distance some young men carrying flour from the mill. Stephen's companions succumbed to temptation.

"Shouldn't we steal their flour?" they said among themselves. "No one can see us. We'll share it and take it to our homes." Everyone agreed, except for Stephen. "It's a sin!" he protested. "And besides, we won't escape justice. We'll be punished as robbers and criminals."

But the others were determined. When their prey approached, they attacked the boys, beat them, and seized the flour.

The young men, beaten and abused, went to their homes and recounted the incident. Afterwards, they notified the governor, Simon Bailo, who sent soldiers to arrest the culprits. The soldiers arrested only Stephen as a suspect, because the others had disappeared. He was walking carefree, confident in his innocence. He honestly explained his situation to the soldiers, but they didn't believe him. They tied him up and put him in prison.

When they brought him before the judge, he again confessed the truth: "I was walking with the robbers, but I took no part in the robbery. You accuse me unjustly."

The judge, however, did not believe him and sentenced him. He asked Stephen, "Which punishment do you prefer: to have your hands cut off or your eyes put out?"

Deeply saddened, Stephen chose the latter, as it seemed less painful to him. With weeping and lamentation, he was

Icon depicting the great miracle of Panagia Cassiopia
in Corfu, Greece in 1530

led to the place of execution, where the terrible sentence was carried out.

Stephen, now unable to move around, was led by his mother. Eighteen miles from the island's capital lay the coastal town of Kassiopi. It was known for a church of the Theotokos, which crowds of people passed by to venerate its miraculous icon. Stephen decided to go to this town. He would stay in the church of the Theotokos and ask for alms from the charitable. He venerated the miraculous icon with his mother and asked the hierodeacon to grant him a small cell for his stay.

The first night they stayed inside the church. His mother, exhausted, fell asleep immediately. He himself, however, could not rest from the pain.

At some point, a light sleep overtook him. He then felt two hands touch him and probe the sockets of his eyes. It was so tangible that he woke up immediately and wondered who could have touched him. And then he saw before him a woman, splendidly dressed and bathed in light. She stood for a moment and then disappeared.

Stephen turned and saw the oil lamps lit. He woke his mother and asked her, "Who lit the lamps?"

"Be quiet and sleep," she told him, thinking her child was dreaming.

But he insisted: "I see the icon of the Theotokos. What I'm telling you are not fantasies!"

Then his mother sat up and looked at his face with anxiety and longing. Indeed, her eyes were not deceiving her. She was witnessing in that moment a vivid miracle: her child's eye sockets were adorned with two blue eyes! Whereas, before the blinding, Stephen's eyes had been black!

Immediately, both mother and son thanked the Most Holy Theotokos with tears of joy for her swift intervention. The noise alerted the church warden monk, who ran to the church to see what was happening. The obvious miracle shook him, and he quickly left for the main town (Chora) to announce the event to the governor.

The governor, perplexed, took Corfu's notables with him and went to visit Stephen. He saw the new eyes in their sockets and marveled. He also saw, as proof, the mark on his eyelids from the red-hot iron. However, the governor still had some internal doubt. For this reason, upon returning to Chora, he summoned the executioner and asked him, "Did you really put out Stephen's eyes, as I ordered?"

"Certainly, I put them out. They are still in a basin. Here!"

Bailo looked apprehensively at the basin. Indeed, inside it were two eyes, and black eyes at that, not blue like the ones Stephen now had. The truth was proven in the most eloquent and convincing way. And the governor, after notifying them to bring Stephen to him, asked for his forgiveness and compensated him with rich gifts. Finally, he diligently renovated the enclosure of the holy church of the Theotokos.

[41]

Panagia Limnia

On a picturesque coast in the northern Euboean Gulf, on the site of ancient Elymnion, the town of Limni is built today. In its magnificent church is treasured the miraculous icon of its patroness, Panagia Limnia.

Around 1560, as tradition preserves, when Suleiman the Magnificent was the sultan, a Turkish ship was sailing in the vicinity of Kassandra heading towards Chalkida. Among the ship's crew was a Christian sailor, the boatswain Demetrios, a pious and elderly man.

Panagia Limnia,
Church of the Nativity of the Virgin Mary in Evia, Greece

The ship was approaching Skiathos, its sails swollen by the Sirocco wind. Suddenly, the wind died down. Then Demetrios gave the order to lower the boats into the sea to tow the ship. At that moment, the boatswain saw a large icon alongside the ship upon the waves. Without wasting time, he descended into a small boat [felucca], lifted the holy icon from the water, and venerated the Panagia depicted on it. Afterwards, he brought the icon onto the deck and handed it over to the captain, the Turk Mehmet.

Immediately, a strong north wind arose, filling the sails. The masts creaked, and the bow cleaved the foamy waves with force. They bypassed the Sporades, entered the Euboean Gulf, and set course for Chalkida. However, as soon as they reached the area of Limni, the wind abruptly stopped, and the ship became immobilized. The boats were launched again into the sea and began to tow it. After hours, they reached the base of Mount Kandili. There, unexpectedly, a storm broke out. The waves rose threateningly and pushed the vessel back towards Limni. As soon as they approached there, the storm ceased, and the sea became calm again.

The crew made another attempt to steer the ship towards its destination. But a new storm broke out, more threatening, pushing them back to Limni again. The captain and the sailors were desperate, unable to discern the hand of the Panagia behind this maritime adventure. Then, finally, the pious boatswain was enlightened. He approached the captain and told him, "We are not going to be rid of this ordeal unless we take the icon of the Panagia ashore here."

The captain agreed and notified the village of Kastria—built a few kilometers away from the coast—to come and receive it. It wasn't long before the faithful people arrived, led by the priests, with processional banners, crosses, and candles. Demetrios was waiting for them on the shore and handed over the sacred icon to them like a priceless treasure.

Immediately, a fresh breeze blew and pushed the sailing ship sternwards with its sailors, straight towards their destination. It was the Panagia's "thank you"; her satisfaction for their trouble.

Meanwhile, the procession started majestically from the beach towards the village. There, in the church of Saint Anna, surrounded by old oak trees, plane trees, and cypresses, they deposited the venerable icon. They chanted the Paraklesis service, a doxology, and thanked the Theotokos for the priceless gift.

The next day, the icon was missing from the church. They searched everywhere for it and found it at the location of present-day Limni. They brought it back to the church of Saint Anna, but it returned to the same place. This happened several times, and thus the inhabitants understood that it was her will to remain there permanently. So they built a small church and placed it inside.

The inhabitants themselves followed the sacred icon; they abandoned Kastria and relocated to Limni. Later, in place of the first small church, they built a magnificent temple and dedicated it to the Nativity of the Theotokos. Every year, on September 8, a celebratory festival takes place in honor of Panagia Limnia.

The dimensions of the icon are ninety-five by sixty-five centimeters. On it is depicted the Panagia Glykophilousa (Sweet-kissing), painted on hard and heavy wood and covered with a silver overlay.

The Panagia Saves Limni from the Germans

A moving miracle occurred during the days of the German occupation, in June 1944. The German detachment that had destroyed Distomo (June 10, 1944), slaughtering over six hundred inhabitants in two days, now crossed over to Euboea. Its purpose was the complete destruction of Limni.

The German storm-troopers reached the entrance of the town. Just then, the German commander saw in the middle of the road a hand blocking the passage of the soldiers, and heard a voice telling him, "This place is mine. You shall not touch it!"

The frightened commander entered Limni and met the authorities. Full of anxiety, he asked to learn who the Protectress of the town was.

"Panagia Limnia," replied the notables. "We have her miraculous icon here, which was found in the sea."

"Only divine power could have thwarted my plans," confessed the commander, and he left Limni without taking action.

The Salvation of a Pious Sailor

The Limnian sailor Evangelos Pantazis recounted the following incident to the parish priests of the town:

> It was December 14, 1960, at 2:30 a.m., and we were sailing in the Bosphorus straits with the ship Pagkosmios Armonia (World Harmony) of the Niarchos company. I was sleeping in my cabin when I heard an otherworldly female voice command: "Jump into the sea!"
>
> I must note that I had special reverence for our Panagia Limnia, and I prayed to her morning and night to protect us. Suddenly, I felt an abrupt jolt. The entire ship shuddered. I looked out the porthole and saw our ship engulfed in flames. We had collided with a Yugoslavian oil tanker carrying fuel oil and

airplane gasoline. From the fierce collision, our bow was cut in half, and the foreign ship suffered a gash twenty meters deep. Meanwhile, I prepared myself and jumped into the sea from the side of European Turkey. While we were swimming, many dolphins around us had formed a cordon, thus protecting us from the sharks that were abundant in the area. For two and a half hours, I battled the waves and finally reached the Turkish coast. Out of the forty-one crew members, only eleven of us were saved.

We attribute our rescue to our Panagia Limnia. That is why we immediately came to Limni, attended liturgy in her holy church, and thanked her for our salvation.

[9]

Panagia Myrtidiotissa (of the Myrtle Tree)

The island of Kythera prides itself on its protectress, "Panagia Myrtidiotissa." Her grace-bestowing icon, majestic and imposing, was discovered, according to tradition, in the "Myrtidia" region, an area then deserted and overgrown with myrtle bushes. A very pious shepherd, while praying, heard in that wilderness a voice saying to him, "If you search around here, you will find my icon. I have been here for a long time, to help this place."

Indeed, within a short time, the shepherd discovered the all-venerable icon of the Panagia amidst branches of myrtle. Moved, he kissed it and carried it to his hut.

The next morning, strangely, the icon had disappeared. He found it again, however, at the spot where he had first discovered it. Exactly there, he built a church, enthroned the holy icon within it, and named it "Myrtidiotissa," because it was found in the "Myrtidia" area and among myrtles.

In the miraculous icon of Myrtidiotissa, the Theotokos is depicted holding the Infant Christ. Her face, as well as the Lord's, is completely dark and framed by pure gold and precious stones. Usually, no features are discernible on them at all. However, at infrequent intervals, the following paradox occurs: the face of the Virgin suddenly changes color and becomes rosy. An inexpressibly sweet smile forms on her lips, while her eyes look upon the faithful with gladness. This lasts for a few seconds, after which her venerable form returns to its usual state.

The Reconstruction

Many years passed since the miraculous discovery of the icon. In 1841, the active hieromonk Agathangelos Kalligeros undertook the struggle for the reconstruction of a new, magnificent church at the sacred pilgrimage site of Myrtidia, completing the work in 1857.

Throughout this period, Myrtidiotissa performed miracles and supported the God-pleasing effort in every way. As soon as the signal was given to start laboring, men, women, and children ran to work at Myrtidia. It is characteristic that during this period absolutely no accident occurred, and not a single bad word, cry, or sigh was heard from the multitude of inhabitants who gathered to work.

Many times, the workers slept outdoors in wintry weather, but no one fell ill; not a head, nor even a finger, ached. They worked with such enthusiasm and willingness that some often forgot to eat and sleep. One person worked as much as ten, and ten as much as a hundred.

During breaks in the work, they formed dances, sang local songs, and chanted hymns to the Theotokos.

One day, the chief workman, who was working high on a scaffold, asked for water. A worker offered him a pitcher, but at the same moment lost his balance and fell from the scaffold. Falling, he cried out, "Dear Myrtidiotissa!" And the Theotokos worked a miracle, because the worker landed standing on the ground unharmed, holding the pitcher full of water.

Once, the workers needed dynamite to break some rocks. In the warehouse, there were barrels full of gunpowder, and the abbot went down himself to take out the necessary quantity. However, the barrels were all found sealed. He didn't have the right tools to open them. Then, absentmindedly, he took an iron rod, heated it in the fire, and, without thinking of the consequences, approached to make a hole in a barrel. At the same moment, a strong blow from an unseen hand knocked him down.

As soon as he recovered, he made the sign of the cross. He reflected with terror on what would have followed if that unseen hand—which was none other than the Panagia's—had not intervened.

The church of Myrtidia is adorned and supported internally by two rows of columns, which are monolithic and made of porous stone. There were no quarries of porous stone on the island, so the master builder chartered a boat and was preparing to travel to arrange their purchase.

Suddenly, a sea storm broke out, lasting fifteen days without interruption. The journey was cancelled. During this time, the master builder's son repeatedly saw in his sleep a venerable woman, dressed in black, telling him, "Go with your father to such-and-such a place, near the church of Myrtidia. In that place, there is an old quarry of porous stone."

And so it happened. The quarry was found, and the quality of the porous stone proved excellent. It is also miraculous that not a single column broke, neither during extraction, nor processing, nor placement inside the church.

Every Saturday, Father Agathangelos had arranged to pay the wages of the workers and artisans. One Saturday, he had no money at all and was preparing to go to the town to borrow some. Before he set off, however, he was informed that money had been found. He went to the money chest, which he had searched shortly before and found empty, and discovered, astonished, two small sacks full of thalers [German silver coins].

Panagia Myrtidiotissa,
Monastery of Panagia Myrtidiotissa,
Kythira, Greece

Another time, payday was approaching again, but there was no money. The artisans and workers were asking for their dues, but the abbot was ill and could not go to the town to borrow. He then fasted for three days and prayed with tears before the icon of the Panagia, asking her to get him out of the impasse.

On the afternoon of the third day, while sitting worried in his cell, he heard a knock on the door. He got up immediately, opened it, but saw no one. He looked around searchingly and discerned someone at a distance coming towards him. He was wearing the old Cretan costume and holding a small sack in each hand.

When he approached Father Agathangelos, he greeted him and said, "I once asked for the help of Myrtidiotissa for an important matter of mine, and I vowed to bring myself to her church a sum of gold and silver coins. The Panagia helped me, but I kept postponing bringing my offering. For the past three days, I have been seeing in my sleep a woman dressed in black and venerable, telling me, 'Go as soon as possible to Kythera, to the church of Myrtidia, to fulfill your promise.'"

After this, the abbot led him to the church. There, after venerating, the Cretan man emptied the two sacks before the astonished eyes of the elder. The church offering plate filled with coins.

When the pilgrim left, Father Agathangelos counted the money. Then he realized with amazement that the amount was exactly what was needed to pay the workers!

The Fishermen

The protection of Myrtidiotissa extends across and embraces the entire island. She heals illnesses, saves from drowning, tames the elements of nature, and anticipates all kinds of incidents and needs.

In February 1892, four fishermen got into a boat in Kapsali, the island's port, and went out into the open sea to fish. It was afternoon and the weather was wonderful. They tried for a long time to catch bait, but failed. Consequently, they couldn't catch any fish either.

Time passed and night fell. At 10 p.m., they were near Antikythera with no results. They decided then to make the return journey. However, the weather began to worsen. A south-westerly wind was blowing, and later a south-easterly. The darkness was thick, and they could no longer distinguish Kapsali, which is why they couldn't realize the change in the weather. They thought they were sailing towards Kapsali, while in reality they were sailing towards Piraeus.

Meanwhile, as the night progressed, the storm grew stronger. The waves rushed relentlessly at the small boat. Due to damage, water began to enter from the hull and threatened immediate sinking.

The unfortunate fishermen threw nets, longlines, and ropes into the sea to lighten the boat's load. The water continued to enter from everywhere. They decided then to carefully break the water pitcher to bail out the water from the boat with it. However, they clumsily broke it, so it couldn't be used. Then they opened holes in the flasks, but the flasks were small and the water in the boat was too much. They soon began to experience the torment of thirst, because the pitcher with fresh water was no longer there.

Desperate from their own efforts, they turned to the Gracious Lady of Myrtidia. They prayed with faith and tears, asking for her help. And she did not delay in answering.

At some point, it seemed to them that they saw at the edge of the boat a venerable woman dressed in black, who immediately disappeared. This vision, although momentary, gave them courage.

"Boys, don't be afraid," shouted the captain. "Myrtidiotissa is with us!"

Immediately the sea calmed, the wind died down, and the fishermen, with thanks and doxologies to the Theotokos, took up the oars. When dawn broke, they realized how much they had deviated from their course. Before them loomed Cape Tainaro. Kythera seemed very far away.

Now a gentle westerly wind began to blow. They raised the sail and set course for their island. The wind grew stronger and stronger, making the vessel fly over the waves. The helmsman could not change direction—a wondrous thing. The direction remained one and the same: the small harbor of Myrtidia.

On the way they crossed paths with the ferry of the line, and the passengers looked at them with surprise and wonder. The wind grew even stronger. Now the boat barely touched the waves. They were rapidly approaching the holy sanctuary of the Panagia.

As soon as they got ashore, they joyfully embraced each other and kissed the rocks of the coast. Immediately, without delay, they started out barefoot for the holy church of Myrtidia. And there, kneeling before the holy icon, they thanked the Mother of God with tears for their unexpected salvation. From then on, every year they followed the procession of the holy icon through the villages of the island, carried it, and spent the night with it at each stop.

The Lightning Bolts

Late at night, on January 21, 1829, the inhabitants of Kythera had long since retired to rest. Suddenly, the silence was broken by the roar of the elements of nature. The floodgates of heaven opened and poured down with a crash, threatening to destroy the island. Lightning seared the firmament, and strong thunder shook the earth to its foundations like volcanoes. The palpable darkness made the night a true hell. And the sea, enraged, opened to the abyss, and then rose like a beast to drown the island. It seemed that impiety and sins had angered the Creator.

High up in the fortress, where many families also lived, a church was built in honor of the Theotokos. At that time, the miraculous icon of Myrtidiotissa was kept inside. While the divine wrath continued, two lightning bolts struck the fortress simultaneously. One broke the flagpole, tore into the church, ripped up the floor, pierced the wall in front of the holy icon, and buried itself in the side room. This space served as a makeshift gunpowder magazine. The lightning, a true fiery snake, ripped the floor here too and overturned the open barrels of gunpowder that were there. Then it came out and met the second lightning bolt, which it had left at the first moment raging in the fortress square. Both together fell upon the governor's mansion, leaving their destructive traces in their wake.

In the fortress, there was also a second large gunpowder magazine. One lightning bolt headed towards it, traversed it, passed between the guard's legs, knocking him down. The guard immediately invoked divine help, and then, as he himself later affirmed, he saw at the church door a woman dressed in white. From this position, the woman—who was nonc othcr than Panagia Myrtidiotissa—ordered the lightning bolts to fall into the sea, which they did. Immediately, the turmoil gave way to unprecedented calm. When dawn broke, all the inhabitants gathered to give thanks to their protectress.

Truly, on that gloomy night, the Panagia intervened with tangible miracles. The lightning bolts overturned so many barrels of gunpowder without them exploding. Also, no human casualties were recorded, only material damage. A litany and procession of the holy icon followed throughout the city with military formation and religious supplications, while the crowd cried out: "Lady Panagia, save us, have mercy!"

The Paralytic

At the end of the sixteenth to the beginning of the seventeenth century, Theodore Koubanios lived in Kousounari, Kythera. According to tradition, he was a descendant of the shepherd who miraculously discovered the venerable icon of Myrtidiotissa, towards whom he nourished special reverence. A good and God-fearing man, he celebrated a festive vigil in the church of Myrtidia every year on September 24—the anniversary of the finding of the precious icon. He went there with his family, offering the necessary items for the Divine Liturgy and the Artoklasia (blessing of the five loaves) service.

Suddenly, Koubanios fell ill. He remained completely paralyzed for many years. However, he did not despair but faced the trial with patience. Since he could no longer go himself, he sent his relatives to Myrtidia every year. The years passed, and the paralytic felt his end approaching. He desired one thing: before he died, to be worthy to venerate the icon of Myrtidiotissa for the last time.

And so it happened. When September 24 came, four of his relatives lifted him on a wooden bed and carried him to Myrtidia. There they laid him before the miraculous icon, full of joy because he was again worthy to venerate it, but also sorrowful for his pitiful condition.

Soon the vigil began. Vespers took place with the Liti (procession with supplicatory prayers), followed by Matins. It was deep night when a pilgrim came out of the church for a moment to rest. Soon, however, he returned to the church and shouted, "Flee quickly, pirates are coming! I clearly heard the noise from the sea. Many must have landed." Pirate raids were so frequent in that era on the island that the pilgrims, as soon as they heard the terrible news, immediately interrupted the vigil and ran to hide.

In their haste, no one thought of the paralytic. Alone and sorrowful, he lay on the bed, abandoned to the mercy of the ruthless pirates. His agony, due to the danger that was ever approaching, had reached its peak. He then lifted his eyes, gazed at the grace-bestowing icon, and with intensified fervor and tears, sought the compassion of the Virgin.

Then the miracle happened: amidst his supplications and laments, he heard a voice from the icon saying to him, "Get up and flee!"

At the same moment, he began to move his hitherto motionless limbs. He stood up, went out of the church, and ran to meet his relatives. At first, he thought he was living in a dream. But when he was assured of his cure, his joy and enthusiasm knew no bounds. At his shouts, everyone came out of their hiding places and surrounded him. And when they heard from his mouth how the paradoxical miracle had happened, they gathered in the church and thanked the Fountain of Compassion with sacred emotion and tears.

Strange, however! The pirates had not yet appeared. Only then did they understand that the noise from the sea was not from pirates, but from divine providence. It was so ordained that the paralytic would remain alone and helpless, pray with faith and fervor, and be deemed worthy of the miraculous cure.

The now-healthy paralytic continued, full of gratitude, to participate even more festively in the celebration of September 24. He even left instructions for his children to continue this blessed custom after his death.

The Punitive Miracle

According to a very ancient custom, the miraculous icon of Myrtidiotissa is carried in procession every year through the villages of Kythera, for the purpose of blessing and sanctification. The tour begins on the Monday of Renewal Week (Bright Week) from the capital and ends on the Wednesday of the week of Thomas Sunday, when it returns to Myrtidia.

One of the first years after the union of the Ionian Islands with Greece, on the Monday of Thomas, the icon was in the church of Holy Unmercenaries in the village of Fatsadika. There, the secretary of the eparchy, Diomidis Fandridis—perhaps eager to flaunt his impiety and disbelief to those present—brazenly approached the sacred icon. Then he scratched the face of the Virgin a little with his fingernail, tapped it with his finger, and said to the faithful, who were terrified by his impious act, "The icon of Myrtidiotissa is nothing more than a piece of wood blackened by age."

This sacrilegious man was invited to a house in the village for lunch. After they sat at the table, Fandridis took a bottle of wine to open it. While he was removing the cork, however, the bottleneck inexplicably broke and deeply wounded the very finger that had impiously scratched the holy icon. The wound caused uncontrollable bleeding. Doctors rushed to offer first aid, but they could not stop the hemorrhage.

Then Fandridis, seeing the immediate danger to his life, abandoned his arrogant attitude and with contrition asked the Panagia to forgive him. Indeed, the Panagia readily forgave him and miraculously stopped the bleeding.

This is the only punitive miracle of Myrtidiotissa, which, however, was aimed at the salvation of a human soul.

The Drought

The scourge of drought had struck the island many times, resulting in dryness. The inhabitants then resorted to the miraculous Myrtidiotissa, carried her holy icon in procession with fervent supplications and tears, and she always sent them rain.

Once, while the people were preparing for such a procession, a wealthy Turk from Crete happened to be present.

"Why this unusual activity around the church?" he asked, puzzled.

"There will be a procession," they informed him. "It hasn't rained on the island for many months. So we will carry the icon of the Panagia in procession so that the divine wrath may cease and the drought may end."

"You are foolish," said the Turk, looking at the sky. "There isn't even a single cloud. However, if it rains after the procession, I will dedicate this diamond-studded jewel to the icon of Myrtidiotissa."

He wagered this golden ornament because he never imagined it could rain.

Soon, clergy and laity processed the miraculous icon. They even knelt and offered prayers with compunction to the Mother of God for the end of the drought. During the procession, clouds began to appear in the sky, continually increasing. When the procession returned to the church, torrential rain began, filling the inhabitants with joy and gladness.

The Turk was left speechless. However, he admitted his defeat and kept his promise. To this day, this golden diamond-studded jewel, in the shape of a crescent moon, adorns the crown of Myrtidiotissa and commemorates that supernatural miracle.

[20]

Panagia Chrysaphitissa

The Byzantine city of Monemvasia, built within the fortress of the peninsula (sixth-seventh century)—the "renowned and cloud-capped" according to the historian Phrantzes—had an adventurous yet also remarkable history, as testified by the surviving ruins of medieval art monuments.

The lower town, built on the slopes of the rock, also had a notable history, as evidenced by the thick walls, the various buildings, and the many churches.

Particularly noteworthy among these is [the church of] Panagia Chrysaphitissa, built in the seventeenth century on the site of another, older church of Panagia Odigitria. Inside it is placed the eponymous miraculous icon of the Panagia, likely a work of the fifteenth-sixteenth century.

According to tradition, the icon was originally located in the village of Chrysapha in Laconia. It arrived in Monemvasia on its own, in a miraculous manner, at the spot where the church and monastery of Panagia Chrysaphitissa were later founded.

The icon was discovered there by an elderly woman, who immediately notified the bishop. Then all the Christians gathered, received it, and processed with it to the metropolitan church, where they placed it.

That same night, the icon disappeared. It returned again miraculously to the place where it was found. After this, the inhabitants built a church there and placed her icon inside it, fulfilling the will of the Theotokos. Below the church gushes a spring, the only one in Monemvasia, whose miraculous water aids in conception, especially of boys.

Meanwhile, the people of Chrysapha learned that the icon was in Monemvasia. So they went and asked for it from the bishop and the rulers. The latter refused to hand

Panagia Chrysaphitissa,
Church of the Panagia Chrysaphitissa, Monemvasia, Greece

it over, at which point the people of Chrysapha resorted to court, claiming their icon. They won the case and returned satisfied to Chrysapha, carrying the icon of the Panagia.

However, she was not pleased with her transfer to Laconia. Therefore, she returned again to Monemvasia, to her newly built church, where she performed exquisite miracles daily. Later, a women's monastery was even founded there.

The Vision of the Abbess

An old manuscript informs us of the following appearance of the Panagia in the monastery of Chrysaphitissa.

It was the fifteenth of August (the Dormition of the Theotokos), and the sisterhood was keeping vigil in the church. At some point, the virtuous abbess Martha saw Mary the Theotokos in a vision. She was seated on a throne and looked at the abbess with kindness and gentleness. The abbess wept for joy throughout the vigil. Towards the end of the doxology, the nuns began to chant loudly. But then the Panagia disappeared.

"Oh, what have you done!" cried the eldress, distressed.

The vigil ended, and the nuns asked the abbess with curiosity what had happened to her.

"During the vigil," she replied, "I had the distinct honor of seeing the Most Holy Theotokos in a vision. But as soon as you raised your voices in the doxology, the Panagia disappeared. Therefore, next time, chant quietly, with a humble voice and a contrite heart. Before a mortal king, everyone stands humble, attentive, and fearful. If one does not maintain such a stance, the king might become angry and dismiss him. Do you understand now how carefully we must stand before the heavenly King, so as not to disturb Him and have Him punish us?"

Punitive Intervention

Panagia Chrysaphitissa continued to work miracles. However, her church soon suffered the calamities of war. The strategic location of Monemvasia, its renowned commercial navy and famous wine, and its wealth and prosperity provoked the powerful of every era, who had turned it into a theater of military conflicts. It endured sieges, plundering, and destruction by pirates, Franks, Catalans, Turko-Albanians, and others.

During a Turkish raid, the church of Chrysaphitissa was looted and turned into a granary. Right next to her holy church lived a Turk, who wanted to expand his house. So he demolished the "catechumena" (women's gallery area) and built baths in that space. The Panagia punished him with the death of all his children.

Additionally, whoever dared to go there to bathe would see before him a woman threatening him. Those who also dared to commit sacrilege inside or outside the church left punished. And they were not healed unless they invited a priest to read a Paraklesis in the church of Chrysaphitissa. For the Panagia worked miracles not only for Christians but also for Muslims.

[41]

Panagia Evangelistria of Mount Helicon

On the slopes of Helicon, where in ancient times the mythical Heliconian Muses were worshipped, stands the monastery of the Evangelistria. Now, the Panagia, "the song of the bodiless," is praised there and worshipped "by bodily voices." Around the holy monastery, age-old plane trees, towering poplars, and pines compose a lush green landscape.

The first church of the monastery, of Byzantine style, was built in the twelfth century, when the Byzantine Empire was at the zenith of its glory. It was later renovated in the seventeenth century, at which time the monastery became stavropegic (directly under the Patriarch). On its unadorned iconostasis is displayed the icon of the Annunciation of the Theotokos, an ancient and miraculous icon, as attested by many testimonies of those who received benefits.

During the period of the national rebirth, numerous stories and legends full of heroism are tied to the tradition of the monastery. The Monastery of the Evangelistria at that time played a national and humanitarian role. It became a refuge for the hunted rayahs (Christian subjects of the Ottoman state) and a hiding place for the heroic chieftains. According to historical accounts, Demetrios Ypsilantis and George Karaiskakis passed through there with their warriors, along with many other fighters.

The Panagia never ceased and does not cease to protect her monastery in every way. The following shocking miracle took place in 1687, when the Greeks had made an attempt to throw off the Turkish yoke.

Among the revolutionaries were the armatoles (militiamen) of Parnassida, Kourmas, and Spanos. These two chieftains attacked and pursued a detachment of Turko-Albanians up to the peaks of Helicon. There, being pressed by other Greek forces, they decided to capture the Monastery of the Evangelistria and fortify themselves within it until reinforcements arrived.

It was dusk. The Turko-Albanians, positioned on the opposite height, saw the monastery's small oil lamp flickering faintly. Following its trembling light, they approached quite close. Then the Serasker (commander) Mukada Pasha

Panagia Evangelistria of Mount Helicon,
Monastery of Panagia Evangelistria, Aliartos, Greece

ordered a group to scout the area, fearing the Greeks might have set an ambush.

When the soldiers reached the turn near the monastery, suddenly a woman dressed in black appeared before them. It was the Most Gracious Lady (the Panagia).

"Leave!" she ordered them. "Return to your positions!"

And saying this, she vanished abruptly, just as she had appeared. It seems the Panagia wanted to protect the women and children, who were in her monastery by the hundreds.

Terrified, the Turko-Albanians returned and recounted the events to their commander. The pasha, angered, ordered the army to set out immediately. Soon they reached the turn. There the Panagia appeared for the second time and prevented Mukada from advancing. Exasperated with anger, he ordered a general attack against the monastery.

Then the great miracle occurred: as the army advanced, the earth opened up and swallowed them whole! The number of Turko-Albanians remains unknown—were there five hundred, or a thousand? Since then, the location was named "Voula," from the sinking (vouliazma) of the Turkish army. Every time they attempt to dig deep at that spot, they find numerous bones, proving that mass burial.

Only two survived from the army—Mukada Pasha and his scribe. The Panagia, in the same form of the black-clad woman, led them to the monastery gate and disappeared.

Deeply moved, the two Turks knelt, and proceeded on their knees into the church. Astonished, they looked at the Panagia of the iconostasis, and in her sweet face, they recognized the woman in black who had led them there.

The miracle of their conversion was thus accomplished. Frightened and repentant, they begged the monks with trembling to keep them in the monastery as servants. Later, the grace of the Panagia completed its work in these two souls. The unbelievers were baptized, and after undergoing the canonical trial period, they became monks and dedicated themselves to the worship of the Evangelistria. Mukada, in fact, showed such good conduct that the brotherhood elected him abbot. And not only did he work and renovate the monastery, but he also donated his vast immovable property to it.

Today, the area of the holy monastery where the "Crucified One" is located is called "the Oratory of Mukada," to commemorate the wondrous events that took place in the era of that repentant Ottoman.

[38]

Panagia Phaneromeni (Revealed)

On Salamis, opposite the Megarian coast "Megalo Pefko," lies the Monastery of Phaneromeni, which was founded in the seventeenth century on the ruins of an old monastery by Saint Lawrence.

When the saint was still a layman named Lambros Kanellos, he saw the Theotokos one night and heard her saying to him, "On the island of Salamis, in the northern part, lies a ruined church of mine. Go, therefore, and rebuild it."

Lambros did not believe the vision. Therefore, the Panagia appeared to him sternly a second and third time, ordering him to obey. So, Lambros set out for the coast, intending to cross to the island by some small boat. However, he encountered a great storm and found no vessel.

While he was sitting pensively, he heard from on high the voice of the Theotokos saying to him, "Throw your cape into the sea, sit on it, and it will carry you safely to the island."

And so it happened. Without hesitation, Lambros climbed onto the cape, crossed the waves, and reached the opposite shore safely.

Source: https://arxon.gr/2017/08/panigyris-ieras-monis-panagias-faner/

Panagia Phaneromeni
Salamis, Greece

There on Salamis, at the spot the Theotokos had indicated, he found the ruins of her church as well as those of an old monastery. Inside the church, there was an icon of the Theotokos, from which the monastery was later named "Phaneromeni" or "Neophanisa" ("Revealed" or "Newly-Revealed").

Lambros rebuilt the church and the cells, stayed there, was tonsured a monk, and with his holy life, he soon became a beacon for laypeople and monks.

The old monastery possessed large landed property, which, however, had been encroached upon by the local inhabitants. The saint struggled and succeeded in reclaiming it. The Panagia herself appeared to him in a vision and indicated to him the boundaries of the encroached lands.

In a short time, he managed to have all the property returned to the monastery. A large olive grove in Glyfada remained, which was held by a very powerful and fanatical Ottoman. The saint went to meet him in person on behalf of the patriarch, but the Ottoman was unyielding.

Then divine justice intervened. The Turk's wife fell gravely ill. Neither doctors nor medicines could cure her. She herself faithfully requested Saint Lawrence to heal her, but the Turk angrily refused. Her condition continually worsened and was rapidly leading her to death.

Only then did the harsh Hagarene summon the saint. And he, after praying, made the sign of the cross on the sick woman's head and healed her. The miracle shook the fanatical Mohammedan, who thanked the saint from the depths of his heart. And not only did he return the olive grove with official documents, but he also offered a respectable sum of money to the monastery.

The Column and the Worker

During the time Saint Lawrence was building the monastery, the Panagia appeared again and told him, "At such-and-such a point on the island lies a stone column buried. Go and bring it to use in the construction."

And so it happened. However, during its transport, the column fell and crushed a worker. The others bent down anxiously to see what had become of him, but the grace of Phaneromeni had performed its miracle. The worker rose safe and unharmed.

The Bishop's Ordeal

At the festival of the Fifteenth of August (Dormition of the Theotokos), a certain bishop, James, from Athens was once present. This bishop, perhaps out of greed, seized the candles and some votive offerings, spoke contemptuously to the saint, and left for the city of Salamis.

That night, he saw the Panagia in his sleep. She was continually stepping on his neck and threateningly telling him, "Quickly send back to the monastery what you stole!"

Terrified, he sent back the stolen items the next day to receive forgiveness from the Theotokos.

Phaneromeni in the National Struggles

During the period of Turkish rule, but also of the national uprising, the Monastery of Phaneromeni became a national center. Within it, women and children, food supplies, ammunition, and various treasures of monasteries, churches, and communities were secured. There the chieftains deliberated on military operations, gathered spoils, and transported the wounded. There were days when the monastery fed seventy-five thousand people!

The chieftains had fortified the monastery, turning it into an impregnable fortress. All Turkish attacks were crushed upon its ramparts. However, the brave defenders did not attribute the victory to themselves, but to the Panagia Phaneromeni, the Champion Leader. This faith of theirs is vividly expressed in the verses that popular muse put into the mouth of the conqueror of Attica, Kyutahi, when he vainly struggled to capture the monastery:

Through villages and countrysides, through mountains and all cloisters
I passed, I trod, I conquered them, I turned them all to ashes.
But Panagia of Koúlouri, the famous monastery,
Which has full threescore semantra, and bells too, three-and-twenty,
With bishops and with presbyters, with chanters ten and fourscore,
She stands and 'gainst me fights alone, does not consent to conquest.
Sixteen were my assaults on her, and twenty-nine my forays,
But lo, her fire burned and scorched, and so I flee, I leave her.

So deep was the reverence of the fighters for Phaneromeni that, after every battle, they deposited the first share of the spoils before her venerable icon. And when they were at the end of their lives, they offered her their most beloved weapons.

Those who were severely wounded in battle asked to be transferred to her monastery, with the unwavering hope that the Panagia would heal them. This deep hope is expressed in the following five verses, which refer to the legendary Karaiskakis:

Although you see me wounded here, my comrades, do not grieve ye.
Swiftly I go to Koúlouri, to the Phaneroméni,
Where are the doctors of the king, that they may heal me wounded;
And there I'll hang my weapons up, upon the holy altar,
And when the priest has blessèd them, I'll put them on and come back.

The years passed. In 1944, some German soldiers, apparently for amusement, were targeting the hermitage of Saint Lawrence from Megalo Pefko with shells. In a short while, they had blown it up, except for the eastern apse of the small church of Prophet Elias.

The Germans ran to investigate the phenomenon. Then they saw in the apse an icon of the Theotokos and an oil lamp that had remained unlit. The soldiers considered it a miracle, so they rebuilt the demolished small church and the cell.

[11]

Panagia Chrysopigi (of the Golden Spring)

In the dance of the Cycladic islands, Sifnos also takes its place, with its gently outlined landscape and the sacred pilgrimage site of Panagia Chrysopigi. This pilgrimage site is built on a wind-beaten cape—some two hundred years before the one in Tinos—and is bound with legends and traditions. Inside the church of the Panagia is kept her miraculous icon, which, as tradition says, was found in the open sea upon the waves. There, in the two eastern cells of Chrysopigi, the poet Aristomenis Provelengios lived a simple life for a large part of his own life, and it was there that he wrote most of his best verses.

Panagia Chrysopigi,
Sifnos, Greece

Many miracles are attributed to Panagia Chrysopigi, which occurred either to individuals or to the entire island. For several years, Sifnos was plagued by locusts. Poisoned bran, petroleum, flamethrowers, and crews for its extermination all proved ineffective. Despair had peaked, but the Panagia had her plan.

In 1929, a good and simple Sifnian woman, Maria Vasalou, had the following dream, which we describe exactly as she narrated it:

> What can I tell you, my child! One evening, I was knitting (with my sock) at a neighbor's house. There, the conversation turned to the locusts that were then ravaging the land. Everyone was saying, "What will become of us with this evil?" (Because, my child, we were then paying people, and they were working day wages to eradicate them, but nothing was happening).
>
> Then I told them, "With these methods we are using, we will achieve nothing." Because—great is her grace—it wasn't many days since I had seen Panagia Chrysopigi in my sleep. She came near me, grabbed me by the sleeve, nudged me, and told me (when I remember it, my son, I shiver all over), "Listen, I will tell you something, and you go and tell them: The locusts, with the way they are fighting them, will never leave unless they bring me out into the middle and carry me around the whole island. And they should also have a liturgy and a blessing of the waters. And then the locusts will rise up like a cloud." And she raised her hands up high, above her shoulders... And the house, my son, and everything around me shone.

The good islander's dream was heeded by the council, and in a few days, a public procession took place. The icon of Chrysopigi was carried around all the villages with utmost reverence and compunction. The next day, there was no trace of locusts on the island. They had all drowned in the sea. The eastern shores were filled with drowned locusts, which the waves washed ashore. Not even a single offspring remained.

[33]

Panagia of Tinos

Scarcely a year had passed since the historic day when Bishop Germanos of Patras raised the banner of the revolution. In the monastery of Kechrovouni, which stands whitewashed on the small island of Tinos, the nun Pelagia, after the evening prayer, retired to her cell to rest. As she had fallen asleep, she suddenly sensed an ineffable fragrance, and immediately heard the door of her cell open with a crash. A majestic woman, who shone like a queen, entered and stood before her bed.

"Get up quickly," she told her. "Go and meet Stamatellos Kagadis, and tell him that my icon has been buried for years in the field of Antonis Doxaras. Let him take care to unearth it and build my house."

The nun awoke terrified, but out of humility, she did not obey the command. The following week, while the nun was praying, she received a second visit from the Panagia in the same place. This time, the Theotokos accompanied her words with a sweet smile, as if to say, "I know your thoughts and hesitations, but do not be afraid. I have chosen you to fulfill my will. So, do not hesitate."

But hesitation still held the good nun captive. Therefore, the Theotokos visited her a third time, on July 29, 1822, once again during prayer. The nun then saw her standing before her motionless and radiating a heavenly light, soft and white. Afterwards, she fixed her gaze upon her and said,

"Pelagia, why did you not obey my command? I repeat it now for the last time."

Terrified, Pelagia mustered all her courage and asked, "Who are you, Lady, who commands me such things and is angry with me?"

Then the Lady seemed to regain her initial sweetness, raised her hand as if pointing to the whole world, and said gracefully, "Evangelize the earth with great joy."

"Praise, O heavens, the glory of God," whispered the nun, falling to her knees.

The bell signaled for Matins. The nun Pelagia got up, made the sign of the cross, and went down to the church. When she narrated her vision to the abbess, the latter listened to her with attention and awe. Finally, she told her, "Pelagia, your vision is divine, and I bless you. Tomorrow morning, act according to the command you received."

The next day, the chosen one of the Panagia set out for Karya, where she met Stamatellos Kagadis. Moved by her story, he referred her to Bishop Gabriel.

The bishop listened tearfully to her account. Afterwards, with a serious and trembling voice, he gave the following explanation: "Your vision, nun, is very important. The Panagia, the Champion Leader, who always protects us, saw our sufferings; that is why she evangelizes to our enslaved nation its liberation from the barbaric yoke. And she reveals her holy icon to us, to strengthen our nation in this struggle."

The bells of the holy church of the Archangels roused the inhabitants. The bishop, with warm words, stirred the people, who, with religious fervor, embarked on the quest to find the icon. They immediately requested permission from Doxaras's wife to begin excavations on his estate. She, however, refused, on the pretense that she did not

Pangia Evangelistria of Tinos (icon discovered in 1823)
Located in the Church of Panagia Evangelistria, Tinos, Greece

have such authorization from her husband, who was away in Constantinople. Besides, the estate was cultivated and therefore should not be destroyed.

That night, she saw a terrible dream. A fierce man in a foustanella (traditional kilt-like garment) threatened that if she did not give permission, he would destroy her. Terrified, she woke up and ran to leave the house. In her confusion, however, instead of opening the room door, she opened the wardrobe and locked herself inside. In the morning, they found her there unconscious. As soon as she recovered, she informed the bishop that not only did she give permission, but she also offered the estate itself for the construction of a church, if the icon were found.

Thus, excavations began on Doxaras's estate in September 1822. Workers from all over the island labored, but the icon was not to be found. Their zeal waned, and in two months, the digging stopped.

Then the Most Gracious Lady intervened with a new miracle to remind the inhabitants of their duty. The wife and sister of Kagadis, whom the Theotokos had specifically indicated for finding the icon, fell gravely ill. This danger made him realize the sacred responsibility he had undertaken from the Theotokos. He therefore hastened to the bishop and begged him to call for a general mobilization of both rulers and people. He was willing to give money himself in order that the excavations could resume.

Indeed, the digging restarted. The villagers worked in shifts, but discouragement once again enveloped them. The great day, however, was approaching. On January 30, 1823, the Phalantadiani were digging in their turn in the field. Around noon, the pickaxe of Demetrios Vlassis struck wood. The pious villager shivered with emotion and, flooded with joy, took the piece he found in his hands. Indeed, he had found the icon, but only half of it, the angel.

Soon they found the other half. A pickaxe had split it in two, yet without damaging the faces at all. The cut, through divine intervention, had been made vertically. The holy icon was cleaned, and the sweet face of the Virgin emerged. It depicts the Annunciation and is a masterpiece of art.

[23]

The Weeping of the Theotokos

In Paşcani, a village in Romania, there is a miraculous icon of the Panagia. This icon was placed in a shrine within the narthex of the village church. On February 15, 1865, the following shocking event occurred:

When the village priest opened the church, he did not find the icon in its usual place. This time, the icon was lying on the ground and weeping so profusely that its tears had drenched the floor. Terrified, the priest closed the church and departed.

The next morning, he found that the icon had moved from the narthex and had positioned itself before the iconostasis, where it was continually weeping. Its mourning lasted for a week and foreshadowed the trials and misfortunes that the country later endured.

[13]

The Turk's Meriem

A copy of the miraculous icon "Axion Estin," brought by refugees to Greece after the persecution of 1922, holds the following wondrous story:

In the years of the Greek Revolution of 1821, shortly before the great catastrophe of Chios, the island was plundered by the Turks. Two Greeks, while fleeing to save

"Axion Estin"[It is Truly Meet] from the Protaton (Athos)

themselves, encountered a Turk. He then gave them an icon, saying, "Take this Meriem (Mary)."

The Greeks hesitated, so the Turk explained, "I tried with an axe to chop it up, to put the boards in the fire. The axe struck the icon many times, but the icon suffered no damage. I looked at it carefully and saw the depicted face smiling at me. I understood that your faith is great and that this icon should not be destroyed. Take it and place it in your church."

The Greeks took it, hid it in a sack, and set off for Reisdere in Asia Minor. The icon was placed in the church of the Monastery of Saint Nicholas, where it quickly became the consolation of the unfortunate and the healer of the infirm. Among its many miracles, we mention the following:

A sick woman asked the Panagia to heal her and vowed to offer her bracelets as a votive gift. Indeed, she recovered. However, the great distance from her home to Reisdere prevented her from fulfilling her promise. Nevertheless, she never ceased to consider her obligation to the Panagia.

One day, she was astonished to find her bracelets missing. She surmised they had been stolen. She then set out to go to the monastery and make up for their value with money. When she arrived, she reported the event to the abbess, who led her before the icon. There, with great astonishment, she saw her two bracelets, which had mysteriously appeared a few days earlier among the other votive offerings. The Panagia had fulfilled the wish of the faithful woman.

[26]

The Blood of the Theotokos

The year was 1922, and the Revolution of 1917 in Russia was now firmly established. The Red partisans (communist rebels) had defeated the Whites (Tsarist rebels) and imposed a new order, abolishing customs and traditions.

In the village of Torginsk, very close to the city of Nerchinsk, they closed the parish church and boarded up its gates with planks. It was a church renowned throughout the Zabaikal region for a miraculous icon of the Theotokos, venerated not only by the Cossacks but also by foreigners.

The church celebrated its feast day on July 8. Crowds of faithful flocked from all over the region. After the Paraklesis, everyone came out of the church and processed with the holy icon through the surrounding villages. Now, however, the procession no longer took place, as the new authority had sealed the church.

That year, a terrible drought had struck the Zabaikal region. The earth cracked from the heat, and the springs, rivers, and wells dried up. The leaves of the trees turned yellow and withered as if fire had passed over them. The crops in the plains dried up.

July 8 was approaching, the day when the Panagia of Torginsk used to be celebrated. On the eve of the feast, at the popular assembly of Torginsk, the white-bearded old Cossacks listened glumly as Stephen Kamenshchikov, a former Red partisan and now village secretary, rambled on:

"Well, comrades," the secretary concluded, "you believe we have a drought because the workers' authority forbade the procession of the Panagia's icon! Because it forbade the wretched priests from dizzying the people, and because it boarded up the church!"

"Exactly!" everyone agreed.

"Stephen!" shouted an old church warden of the Torginsk church. "This year we wish to process with the icon of the Panagia in our fields. Nothing bad will happen. Ask for permission from the authorities."

19th century copy of the Abalak Icon of the Mother of God "The Sign"

The Panagia of Torginsk icon was likely one of the early copies of the Abalak (Abalatskaya) Icon of the Mother of God "The Sign," which was painted in 1636. In addition to the Mother of God with the Child, the Torginskaya icon also depicted Saints Nicholas and Mary of Egypt. Unfortunately, the Panagia of Torginsk icon was lost in 1938, and the original 1636 Abalak icon has not survived.

"Alright comrades," replied the secretary. "Since you insist so much, I will act according to your wish. However, don't expect rain. Thus, you will understand in practice that God does not exist."

The request was made by the secretary and the answer came back positive from the members of the G.P.U. [State Political Directorate – a Soviet secret police agency]. The joyful news that they would celebrate again like in the good old days and process with the miraculous icon in the fields for rain spread like lightning.

The next morning, a multitude of people had flooded the church and the surrounding area. Everyone arrived dressed in their festive clothes, while the bell ringing complemented the celebratory tone of the day. The only discordant note was the presence of the G.P.U. agents with their caps and ironic expressions.

Soon, white-bearded Cossacks emerged from the church carrying the heavy reliquary with the icon of the Theotokos. The priests followed in their gold-embroidered vestments.

The people knelt. Everyone's eyes were tearful. The large icon with the precious jewels and the radiant eyes of the Theotokos passed before the faithful. At some point, those radiant eyes met the gloomy gaze of Kamenshchikov and startled him. He felt them looking into the depths of his soul. But he acted indifferent. He adjusted his cap and started smoking.

The Paraklesis had begun, and the elderly Father John slowly and clearly pronounced the petitions:

"Grant rain to the thirsty land, O Savior!"

How people and nature longed for the beneficial rain! The unbearable heat at that moment reached the point of madness. The priests sprinkled the yellowed wheat and the parched earth with holy water.

Until evening, they processed with the icon of the Theotokos through all the fields and made continuous supplications, while the crowd followed tirelessly over hills, roads, and slopes.

Kamenshchikov, riding his horse, smiled ironically. At some point, he threw away his cigarette and muttered angrily, "I'll show you who your Christ and your Panagia are."

Now the procession approached the houses of the village of Torginsk. Exactly in the middle stood Kamenshchikov's house. At the door, his elderly mother waited reverently.

"Old woman!" he shouted at her. "Don't you dare bring that gypsy woman into our yard!"

"What words are these, Stephen! Have you gone mad?" she protested.

Meanwhile, small clouds appeared in the sky, continually growing larger. At some point, the priest stopped for the usual prayer. Then Stephen, flushed red, ran towards him shouting, "Enough with the comedy! Comrades, surround this old box! Now I'll show you that there is no God and no Panagia."

And saying this, he grabbed Father John by the beard and pushed him forcefully. The white-haired priest rolled on the ground, while the golden cross he was holding slipped from his hand. Kamenshchikov kicked the cross with his boot, then drew his sabre and struck the frame of the icon with all his might.

The crowd was agitated. A moment passed, and then cries were heard:

"Blood, blood!"

"Miracle, miracle!"

Stephen looked around fiercely. "Why are they shouting?" he wondered.

"Stephen!" his mother shouted furiously. "Mortal sin! Look at the Lady!"

He glanced at the icon and froze. From the right cheek of the Theotokos, blood was trickling drop by drop. It ran downwards and stained her silver covering purple.

Suddenly, as if with a foreign voice, Kamenshchikov himself shouted, "Tears, tears!"

From the large eyes of the Panagia, large tears, clear as diamonds, were streaming. And immediately, the blessed rain began to fall from the sky.

It rained continuously for three days. The soaking rain fell incessantly on the thirsty earth, and it greedily drank the life-giving water. On the fourth day, a brilliant sun rose in the sky. It shone, showing people the miracle of life and renewal. The Panagia of Torginsk had performed her miracle.

The members of the G.P.U., humbled by their setback, sealed the church again and took the holy icon away to a distant city.

The greatest miracle, however, occurred in Kamenshchikov, in that atheist Bolshevik. The Panagia, with her blood and tears, watered his faithless but thirsty soul, and it did not take long for it to bear the fruit of faith and repentance.

Years passed. On an autumn night in 1930, a small mounted detachment of White partisans silently entered Torginsk. In the center of the village, they stopped, removed their caps, and crossed themselves. The leader, his voice broken with emotion, began to say, "At this spot, comrades, once stood the famous church of the Panagia of Torginsk. Now there is nothing but this black plowed field. Eight years ago, I was an eyewitness to the last miracle her grace performed. Since that day, shocked by my unheard-of sacrilege against her holy icon, I found no rest anywhere. Those radiant eyes, that living blood and tears on her face, followed me everywhere. And they became the cause of my conversion. I, Stephen Kamenshchikov, the atheist Bolshevik and persecutor of Orthodoxy, have now become a faithful Christian. Now, my dear ones, as you know, the Soviet authorities have placed a huge bounty on my head, as well as on yours. Now we all understand what Russian reality means, and what it means to bear the cross of the Lord."

Stephen fell silent. He spurred his horse, and they all set off for his ancestral home. He wished to see his mother after eight years of separation. He entered the yard and proceeded to the porch, unaware that death was lurking for him. But the radiant eyes of the Panagia watched over him and would avert the danger. The floorboards creaked under his feet. He lifted the latch and knocked loudly on the door.

"Who is it?" a voice was heard.

"It's me, mother, Stephen!" he replied softly.

"Stephen, my beloved child!"

The door opened, and the mother fell eagerly into her son's embrace. But immediately she pushed him away, gesturing with her hands and stifling her sobs.

Stephen did not understand. He stood stunned on the dark porch.

"Ambush!" the old woman cried wildly. "Flee quickly! The villains have been waiting for you here since evening. Someone close to you betrayed you."

"Old hag!" a voice was heard. "You betrayed us!"

And immediately three pistol shots rang out. The mother collapsed, covered in blood, as her son jumped outside. His comrades rushed into the yard.

"Grenades!" Stephen roared.

Dozens of grenades were thrown at once at the open door and windows. The house shook from the explosions. G.P.U. men ran to cut off the partisans' retreat, but they were already outside the village. Far off, the galloping of horses and gunshots could be heard. Then all fell silent. It was still night, and the moon made the waters of the Torga river sparkle.

In the summer of 1932, the train stopped at the station of Harbin, in Manchuria, China. Among those disembarking was a man of medium height, wearing a grey hat and carrying a suitcase. It was Stephen Kamenshchikov, who managed to escape from Russia to China. Although he had fled abroad, his spirit had not been broken. He believed that soon he would again be useful to his beloved homeland, where he would someday return to repay his imprescriptible debt to the Most Holy Theotokos.

[31]

Panagia of Skripou

In September 1943, following the surrender of the Italians, a group of inhabitants from Orchomenos, Boeotia, approached the railway station of Livadia. They demanded that the Italian garrison there surrender its weaponry. Otherwise, they threatened them with an attack by the partisans located in the area of Tzamali (Dionysos).

The Italians refused to surrender and informed the Germans, who decided to burn Orchomenos and punish the inhabitants.

On the night of September 9, the Germans entered Orchomenos and arrested six hundred hostages. One detachment remained in the city, while another with three tanks advances towards Dionysos.

Just outside Orchomenos is the oldest church in Boeotia (built in 874 AD), dedicated to the Dormition of the Theotokos—the old monastery of Skripou.

It was still midnight, and the phalanx had passed the church by five hundred and fifty meters when suddenly the first tank stopped in the middle of the road. Before them,

Icon depicting the miraculous intercession of
the Mother of God of Skripou

the Germans saw a majestic woman with her hand raised in a prohibitive gesture.

The second tank tried to overtake the first but fell into a ditch, while the third tank immobilized itself in a field through which it was trying to pass.

Dawn broke on September 10. The German commander, Hoffman, asked the inhabitants for a tractor to pull the tanks. Then something wondrous happened. These heavy tanks were moved by the tractor like empty matchboxes!

"Miracle, miracle!" shouted the commander and asked the inhabitants to take him to the church.

They led him to the church, and the German recognized, in the icon of the Theotokos on the iconostasis, the woman who had prevented the phalanx from advancing! He immediately fell to his knees and shouted with admiration, "This woman saved you! Honor her and glorify her."

Orchomenos was saved. Hoffman ordered the six hundred condemned men to be freed and promised that, until the end of the war, the city would suffer no harm. The inhabitants thanked and glorified their protectress, the Theotokos, for their unexpected salvation.

The sun was setting. The tanks departed with their cannons lowered, because they had been defeated by the Champion Leader of Orchomenos. Since then, September 10 has been established as a day of celebration. As long as Hoffman lived, he himself attended the festival almost every year. He even dedicated a large oil lamp to the Panagia and financed the first depiction of the miracle.

[7]

Panagia Spiliotissa

In the Monastery of Spilia in Agrafa, there is a miraculous icon of the Panagia, which was found in 1904 in a wondrous manner by the brothers Athanasius and Parthenius. During the years of Turkish rule, the entire Thessalian plain had bowed to the Turk. But in the Monastery of Panagia Spiliotissa, perched like an eagle's nest on an inaccessible peak of Agrafa, the conqueror had not set foot.

To reach the monastery, one had to traverse a downhill path, steep and sloping, barely wide enough for one person. Below, the abyss yawned.

At the monastery's feast, on the fifteenth of August (the Dormition of the Theotokos), some pious pilgrims would see the Panagia herself. They would see her standing immensely tall at the edge of the cliff with open hands, a wall for those who went to honor her, lest anyone slip into the abyss. They also say that no one was ever lost from among those who journeyed there.

The monastery had become a thorn in the side of the infidels. It was a constant vexation to them. The entire Turkish force stumbling over a few stones and walls!

But how could they reach there? Besides the arduous journey—it was a two-day trek from Mouzaki through unknown and inhospitable parts—they had to pass that precipitous path. And what if someone were to roll down the slope, dragging others with him, causing panic and the loss of the Janissaries?

They thought of blockading them. But how long would they hold out? Winter would come, a man's height of snow would fall, and they would have to leave. Then those goat-like men from the surrounding villages would climb from elsewhere and reach there. Not to mention that the monastery's cellars would be full. And those dogs fasted to the point of death most days of the year. It wouldn't bother them a bit if they were besieged.

So, they sent a message to the monks of Spilia—something they had done before—to come and submit,

Panagia Spiliotissa
Panagia Spilia Monastery, Agrafa, Greece

to surrender. But to no avail. Even the bishop sent them a message to come down and submit, while of course keeping their faith, but they replied, "Holy Bishop, we feel for you and understand you. Your path is a Golgotha. Do your duty, and let us do ours."

Finally, the Turks decided to attack them. One morning, the monks found themselves surrounded by the infidels.

"Open up!" they shouted. "We are friends. We will enter as visitors."

"Her grace does not accept infidels," replied the monks.

Then they barred the doors, fortified themselves, and the battle began. The ravines echoed with the gunfire. At some point, however, the heavy doors gave way, and the Hagarenes rushed in with shouts. The monks no longer had rifles, bullets, or gunpowder. They grabbed knives, wood, and stones. The struggle was unequal, and blood soon stained their worn and dusty robes.

The abbot was in the sanctuary at that hour, performing the final part of the liturgy. The infidels seized him, tied him up, and tortured him. Then they burned and trampled the holy icons and went and brought the holy chalice, which still contained the Holy Communion. A Turk then grabbed it and threw it down the cliff.

"Dog!" screamed the elder, his eyes filling with tears. A scimitar flashed in the air and, on its descent, cut off the abbot's head.

For three days, the Janissaries reveled in their victory. And when they tired of reveling, they set off for the plain. The news of the destruction fell upon the region like a thunderbolt.

"The Turks have taken the Monastery of the Panagia!"

"And a miracle?"

"No miracle."

"Nothing?"

"Nothing."

"Glorified be your name, O Most Gracious Lady."

The dead bodies of the monks remained unburied. No one dared to approach. Only the priests in the villages secretly read Trisagion prayers for the souls of the ethno-martyrs.

At some point, however, the bravest among them journeyed up to the monastery. They arrived in the afternoon. They had a priest with them. Their hearts tightened as soon as they saw the slain. They washed the wounds, placed them in the church, and kept vigil over them through the night. In the morning, they kissed them all and then buried them. They rang the bell mournfully and set off for their villages.

The monastery closed. Who knew if it would have remained closed forever! But in their hearts, a spark of hope secretly burned.

Years passed. One evening, a shepherd boy was grazing his sheep on a mountainside. Suddenly, as he was lost in the reverie of the night, he saw a light in the depths of the ravine. He was puzzled. What could it be? He rubbed his eyes and looked again. It looked like a large oil lamp.

He notified the villagers, and one morning about ten of them went down into the ravine together. A priest went with them. When they approached, they stopped short. A fragrance wafted around them. They crossed themselves and proceeded. And then, what did they see!

Ahead, upon a smooth stone, was, as if wedged, the holy chalice. It was the chalice of Spilia. Inside it, untouched, the last Communion—which the abbot had not had time to consume—gave off a sweet scent.

The priest trembled. All of them were now weeping. They were witnesses to a miracle.

The priest reverently lifted the chalice, and they began the ascent. The shepherd boy flew up, notified the village, and they rang the bell joyfully. Then they came out to meet them.

The next day, they all set off for the monastery. The priests in their splendid vestments, the processional fans, the censers, and a great crowd of people. There they deposited the holy chalice, celebrated the Divine Liturgy, and glorified Panagia Spiliotissa for her miracle.

From that day, the shepherd boy remained at the monastery and reopened it after the destruction. He had been chosen by the Panagia. He became a monk, and when later Spilia was filled with monks, he was a virtuous and enlightened abbot. And he never ceased to narrate with simplicity and humility the miracle he was deemed worthy to see. Since then, the Panagia always performs some miracle at her feast.

[22]

Panagia Prousiotissa

High on the fir-covered mountain peaks of southwestern Evrytania, and wedged between vertical, grayish rocks with wild majesty, emerges the holy monastery of Proussos.

It is a stavropegic and historic monastery, with magnificent three-story buildings. Among them exists a hewn cave, which houses in its interior the first and old church of the monastery. Within this is kept the miraculous icon of the Panagia, which is called Prousiotissa.

According to tradition, this icon was originally placed in a church in Proussa. During the years of iconoclasm (829 AD), a certain nobleman took charge of it, intending to transfer it to Greece for safety. However, when he reached Kallipoli, he lost the icon, which then miraculously made its way to the spot where the monastery of Proussos is located today. The event soon became widely known. It was not long before it also reached the ears of the nobleman who was transporting it. He ran, recognized it with emotion, was tonsured a monk there, and is considered the first founder of the monastery.

The German's Punishment

In the history of the monastery, it is mentioned that it was destroyed many times during the Turkish occupation. The last destruction, however, which reduced the buildings to heaps of ruins, was carried out in 1944 by the Germans.

After the destruction of the buildings, an officer wanted to burn the church as well. He tried many times, but without success. While he was standing outside giving orders, he was exemplarily punished by the hand of the Panagia. An invisible force threw him violently onto the paved stones. The blow was powerful, and the German was unable to rise. The soldiers lifted him and put him on an animal to transport him to Agrinio.

Thus, the church remained unharmed, just as it has been preserved intact throughout the centuries.

The Unknown Nun

Four years passed. The civil war was raging in the Greek countryside. The inhabitants of Evrytania and mountainous Nafpaktia abandoned their villages and sought refuge for safety in other parts of Greece. Along with them, the miraculous icon of the Panagia also became a refugee. It too followed the fate of its children and was transported by the monks of Proussos to the metropolis of Nafpaktos. The monastery remained completely deserted.

After some time, army operations began. The ninth division undertook clearing operations in Evrytania. Some units passed through Proussos. Certain officers and soldiers approached the dark little church in the cave and entered to venerate.

Panagia Prousiotissa,
Proussos, Greece

Therein they beheld a strange sight: before the iconostasis, to the left of the beautiful gate, a lit oil lamp and a nun kneeling.

The soldiers were puzzled. How was this nun living here, at a time when Evrytania was completely deserted by inhabitants? How was she sustained, what did she eat, where did she find oil for the lamp? So they asked her, and she modestly and sorrowfully answered them, "My children, I have been living here, all alone, for two and a half years now. For my own life, food and bread are not needed. It is enough for me that I have my oil lamp lit."

The soldiers, tired from the operations and in a hurry to leave, paid no attention to her words. The next day, however, when they recalled them, they understood that it was something miraculous. And when, later, they were passing through Nafpaktos, they persistently asked their commander for permission to visit the metropolitan.

The Bishop of Nafpaktia and Evrytania, Christopher, received them with love, and after listening to them with emotion, shed light on the mystery.

"The church you visited," he told them, "belongs to the now deserted Holy Monastery of Prousiotissa, whose miraculous icon has been here for over two years, in the chapel of our metropolis, in Saint Dionysios. Go and venerate it, and you will understand."

They indeed went and venerated. Then, spontaneously, the explanation for their query was given to each one: in the icon of the Theotokos, they recognized that nun whom they had met in the little church of the cave, high up in Proussos!

[15]

Panagia Malevi

Parnonas, the verdant mountain of Kynouria with its many monasteries, hosts on its northern side the Holy Monastery of Panagia Malevi.

The icon of the Dormition of the Theotokos, which is kept there—myrrh-gushing and miraculous—has captivated the entire Greek nation in recent decades. The holy myrrh gushes forth fragrant from the holy icon. Often it is so abundant that it flows down the icon stand and reaches the floor of the church.

The Woman with the Myrrh

The late lay preacher Demetrios Panagopoulos, who contributed greatly to the dissemination of this wondrous event, recounted his impressive acquaintance with the holy myrrh and the Monastery of Malevi:

> After the end of one of my talks, a certain unknown woman dressed in black approached me. She held in her hand a white envelope with a good amount of cotton, which exuded an unprecedented fragrance. She offered it to me and said, "Mr. Panagopoulos, this is cotton with holy myrrh from the miraculous icon of the Panagia of the Malevi Monastery, which is located in Astros, Kynouria. They send it to you as a blessing and await your visit." I took it, kissed it, and smelled it. I felt an unusual and indescribable fragrance.
>
> Exactly one year later, an unknown woman dressed in black approached me again after my talk, offering me and repeating what she had said the first time. The third year after, the same thing happened

again. Then, as if I awoke from a lethargy, I wondered who this woman could be who had visited me for the third time already!

In 1970, I was deemed worthy to make a pilgrimage to the Monastery of Malevi. Even before I entered the monastery, I was greeted by that heavenly aroma which, three years earlier, I had smelled from the cotton of the black-clad woman.

My emotion that evening at the monastery was indescribable. After this, I equipped myself with photographs and kept notes about the monastery and the sacred icon, with the purpose of also helping in the dissemination of the wondrous event.

The Healing of the Novice Nun

Among the many and varied miracles performed by the grace of Panagia Malevi, the healing of the novice nun Veronica, in the monastery of Saint John the Theologian, in the settlement of Papagou, is characteristic:

Veronica suffered from cancer. She had been hospitalized many times in the Voula hospital. Finally, she returned to her monastery, paralyzed in her hands and feet, to die there.

The nuns agreed that she should be tonsured a great-schema nun on Wednesday, March 8, 1970, so that she might depart as a nun. The doctor, however, did not give much hope for her life, so it was decided that the tonsure would take place on Sunday, March 5, at Vespers. They would carry her to the church in their arms, on an armchair. A certain lady prepared her monastic habit and put an amulet on her, which also contained cotton soaked with the myrrh of Malevi.

Myrrh Streaming Icon of the Dormition of the Theotokos (Panagia Malevi), Monastery of Panagia Malevi, Mount Parnonas, Greece

On Thursday, Friday, and Saturday, the sick woman was in a state of aphasia. On Saturday, she suffered all day from terrible pains. In the afternoon, she managed to ask for a pain-relieving injection, which allowed her to sleep.

While she was sleeping, she heard at some point a discreet knock on the door.

"Who is it?" she whispered with evident displeasure. "They won't let me rest!"

Then she saw the door open and three people enter the cell: a beautiful and majestic lady, a bishop, and another official person, who wore a chiton.

As she looked at them astonished, the lady spoke and said, "You are wondering, of course, who we are and whence we are coming at such an hour. I am from the monastery of Malevi, and from there I come. His Eminence here stays in Aegina. (Apparently, it was Saint Nektarios). From here is the beloved disciple of our Lord, who is your protector and stays here. (Apparently, Saint John the Theologian). I had intended to come after a few days, to visit you. However, I thought it better to come tonight, since you will become a nun tomorrow, to help you get up, to make you well, so that you can perform your duties and slowly your little tasks and everything."

"My lady," replied Veronica, "I cannot stand on my feet, I cannot move. Two or three sisters come to lift me, and still, they cannot make me well."

"Do you believe in the power of God?" asked the lady.

"I believe."

"What is impossible with men is possible with God."

Then she took an icon that was in the cell (the icon was of Panagia Malevi), gave it to the novice, and told her, "Here, take this so you may understand who I am."

Then the sick woman recovered her senses and cried out, "My Panagia, is it you?"

And the Panagia, after smiling at her, disappeared along with her retinue, leaving the sister healed.

The first to experience the miracle was the nun Nektaria, who was serving her, and she ran to announce it in the church, for it was the hour of Vespers. Sorrow was immediately succeeded by joy. Bell ringing, tears of joy, doxology, Salutations to the Theotokos, and Artoklasia followed.

On the afternoon of the following day, amidst an unprecedented crowd and moving demonstrations, the monastic tonsure took place with the only difference being that Veronica, who was renamed Sister Magdalena, was not sitting paralyzed in the chair, but was standing upright and healthy.

[30]

Miracle at the Camp

Father John Chakos, a priest of the Greek Orthodox Diocese of Pittsburgh in North America, recounts a contemporary miracle of the Theotokos, which took place at a camp:

Every year, for eight years now, I spend a week of the summer as chaplain at our diocese's camps. I work with children aged 13-18, along with other clergy, with the aim of offering the campers various spiritual opportunities: talks, counsel, confession, group discussions, prayer, and sacred services.

On Sunday, July 17, 1988, the weekly camp session began, and children and group leaders gathered from various parts of the Diocese of Pittsburgh.

On Tuesday evening, we had the so-called "saints' night." That evening, one child from each group recounted to all the campers the life of a saint. As the night progressed, more and more campers stood up and, in an atmosphere vibrant with emotion, narrated miracles they had seen or heard.

On Thursday afternoon, we chanted the Paraklesis to the Panagia. Fathers Terrence Linos, Michael Varvarelis, and I presided. At the end, I anointed all the children, using cotton moistened with tears from the miraculous weeping icon of the Panagia of Chicago. This icon is located on the iconostasis of the holy church of Saint Nicholas, of the Albanian Orthodox parish of Chicago. It began to weep on December 6, 1986, and stopped in July 1987, after performing many great miracles for Orthodox and non-Orthodox alike. At the end, Father Terrence Linos brought me a framed photograph of this icon to bless. I passed the lightly moistened cotton over the glass, forming the sign of the cross.

On Friday morning, a talk was given at the general assembly of the camp about what the Holy Spirit can do in us. On the occasion of this talk, the

Photos of the weeping icons from Camp Nazareth
(Photo credit to John Conomos)

girls of Saint Markella's cabin, whose feast day it was, united their prayers and asked the Holy Spirit to show them a sign on that day, as their group was celebrating. One camper even asked, 'Why can't we too see a miracle in our lives?'

On Friday afternoon, all the children were preparing for the evening talent show and national dances. Two hundred visitors gathered at the camp grounds to watch the event, as it was visiting day.

Precisely at the moment the skits were to begin, a female group leader, Effie Hatzi, came running to me. She was very distraught. She took me aside and explained with tears in her eyes that in cabin 3, an icon of the Panagia was weeping. I immediately ran there and saw, leaning against the screen of a window, the icon I had blessed the previous day after the Paraklesis. It was the copy of the Panagia of Chicago. Before it, some female group leaders were kneeling, visibly moved.

Indeed, from the eyes of the Panagia, small drops like tears were rolling downwards. I knelt reverently and prayed along with the others. I added my own tears to those of the Panagia. After a brief quandary, I returned to the pavilion, where the skits had already begun. I announced the miracle to the visitors and invited them to come and venerate.

While the Paraklesis was being chanted in the area of the miracle, Father Terrence anointed those approaching with cotton soaked in oil and tears from the icon of the Panagia. A strong aroma permeated the atmosphere. Those who had been anointed smelled it more distinctly, because it originated from the substance with which they had been blessed. A camper from Lorain, Ohio, brought his own icon to Father Terrence to bless.

An hour might have passed since the wondrous event when Effie Hatzi came to announce a second miracle that had now occurred in cabin 7. The icon of the child from Lorain was also weeping and exuded a strong fragrance. As I observed, small oily drops had formed at the point where the icon had been anointed by Father Terrence. However, the amount of liquid that had appeared could in no way be attributed to the touch of a piece of cotton.

We transferred this second weeping icon to the chapel, just like the first, where many campers came for a vigil and prayer. The sweet fragrance that was first noticed in the cabins and on the icons became very intense in the church. It was so pervasive that I could literally taste it in my mouth. Some sensed the fragrance even in the outdoor areas, as far as the fence of the parking area, which was fifty meters away from the chapel.

New visitors continually arrived as soon as they learned the amazing news. During the night, the campers brought various icons of paper, wood, and canvas to be blessed. On some of these, the same wondrous phenomenon manifested: the tears and the fragrance.

Father Michael Rosco, the director of Camp Nazareth, distributed several pamphlets that had on the cover a photograph of the weeping icon of Chicago. Some of these, after being blessed, exhibited the same wondrous properties. One pamphlet is worth recalling: I saw on its cover tears like beads, which were forming on their own on the eyes of the

Panagia and the divine Child, quite far from the place where the sign of the cross had been made.

By the end of the vigil, I had counted a total of nineteen icons that had reproduced the fragrant tears.

I understand that all this is hard to believe. The witnesses to these miracles, however, are many, at least two hundred: campers, group leaders, visitors, eight priests, and two bishops. All of them recognize it as a miracle, connected with the miraculous icon of Chicago. Others may not agree, nor are they obliged to. For us who believe, however, the myrrh-scented tears gush forth from the heart of a compassionate Mother, who intercedes for the healing of a world sick from sin.

[37]

PART II

UNMERCENARY PHYSICIAN

St. John of Damascus (16th century fresco)
All Saints Church Monastery of Varlaam Katholikon,
Meteora, Greece

Saint John of Damascus

Saint John of Damascus lived during the reigns of Emperor Leo III the Isaurian (717-741) and his successor Constantine Copronymus. His homeland was Damascus in Syria, then the seat of the Arab Caliphate. His parents, prominent Greco-Syrians, were numbered among the few Christians in the city. His father, Sergius, was a minister in the Caliph's government, responsible for the affairs of the Christians.

According to tradition, the saint pursued his general education under the wise teacher Cosmas, a captive Greek monk from Italy. With his sharp intellect and diligence, he soon acquired a thorough education, as is evident from his writings.

After his father's death, he too entered the service of the Caliphate as chief counselor. With the declaration of Iconoclasm by Leo the Isaurian, John engaged with his pen in the struggle for the holy icons. With the "sword of the Spirit," he denounced Leo's dogma. He substantiated his positions with theological proofs, historical evidence, and hagiographical examples, and called the iconoclasts heretics and enemies of God.

Leo sought revenge. He forged a letter from John and sent it to the Caliph of Damascus. In this letter, the saint supposedly asked the emperor to rescue him from the Caliph's hands. The enraged ruler summoned John and, without allowing him to defend himself, ordered his right hand to be cut off. Soon, that sacred hand which denounced the iconoclasts was cut off and, stained with its blood, was hung in the marketplace for public display.

In the evening, the saint sent mediators and asked for his hand back to bury it. As soon as they brought it, he took it and went to the small church he had in his house. He approached the icon of the Most Holy Theotokos, fell face down on the ground, placed the severed hand in its position, and pleaded and lamented and groaned:

> *O Sovereign Lady, all-pure one, O Mother of my Lord God,*
> *My right hand was severed for the venerable icons.*
> *Thou knowest surely the cause for which was Leo wrathful.*
> *Hasten, therefore, and speedily restore my hand, I pray thee.*
> *The right hand of the Fashioner, who took from thee His body,*
> *Works many wonders when entreated by thy supplication.*
> *So now do thou restore and heal my severed hand, the right one,*
> *So that it might compose thee hymns with harmony and rhythm,*
> *As many as thou grant me to compose for thee, my Lady,*
> *And for thy Son and the defense of the Orthodox Faith.*
> *Whatever askest thou of God, thou gainest as His Mother!*

Thus spoke the saint with tears and fell asleep. He then saw the Mother of God in her icon, looking at him with serenity and compassionately telling him, "Look! Your hand is healed. Do not grieve anymore. But make it, as you promised me, 'the pen of a swiftly writing scribe.'"

John awoke and saw with astonishment his hand healed and reattached. His joy was so great that all that night he sang praises and thanks to the Panagia.

The miraculous healing profoundly shook him and led him to a great decision. He freed his slaves, distributed his property, and set out, free from all worldly cares, for the Monastery of Saint Savvas with the intention of becoming a monk.

There he displayed unparalleled obedience and humility to his elder. He did nothing without his blessing. Once, however, his neighboring monk pressured him to write a funeral hymn. He composed the troparion "All human things are vanity..." and chanted it with compunction in his cell.

The elder happened to hear him. And because he had forbidden him to write and chant, he assigned him the penance of cleaning all the latrines of the monastery. John obeyed willingly, starting with the latrine of the monk who lived in the adjacent cell.

A few days later, the Most Holy Theotokos appeared to the elder while he was sleeping and said to him, "Why did you block such a spring that gushes forth heavenly nectar? Let it flow, to water the entire inhabited world. John will surpass the lyre of David, he will compose hymns better than the ode of Moses, and will sing more artfully than Orpheus. He will denounce heresies and rightly divide the dogmas of the faith."

From then on, the saint, now with the blessing of his elder, like a spiritual torrent, began to chant, write verses, compose melodies, and write for the glory of God, His Mother the Panagia, and the saints. And when "he had finished the work which the Lord had given him to do," he departed to heaven, to enjoy there the manifold reward of his labors.

[41]

The Abscess of the Schoolmaster

Eugene Voulgaris served as director of the Athonite Academy in the latter half of the eighteenth century. In the holy Monastery of Dionysiou, this wise man experienced the miraculous power of the Panagia of the Akathist Hymn, who healed him of a painful abscess. He noted:

> I will narrate the miracle the Panagia performed for me, thereby expressing the gratitude I owe her. I am not writing this to boast that I supposedly received a divine visitation, nor does it bother me if I am characterized as foolish for this account.
>
> In 1758, then, I was the schoolmaster at the Athonite Academy. When spring came, a dangerous abscess appeared deep in my left armpit. I suffered from a slight fever and felt exhaustion. The abscess continually grew larger and hardened. The entire hollow of the armpit and the left breast had hardened like stone. I was in terrible pain. I could not only not stand, but not even sit, lie down, sleep, or breathe freely. I felt despair and preferred death to that terrible suffering.
>
> Some friends advised me to seek treatment in a hospital in Chios, Smyrna, or Thessaloniki. However, any movement was difficult and dangerous.
>
> In my despair, I learned that a certain Dionysiou monk, Nicephorus, was an expert in operating on abscesses. I decided to visit him. They put me with great difficulty into a small boat, and after circumnavigating Athos, we arrived at the Monastery of Dionysiou.
>
> Father Nicephorus carefully examined the abscess and said to me, "Have courage. But expect the cure from the Honorable Forerunner, the patron of the monastery. I will only serve as his assistant." At the same time, he applied emollients to the painful area to soften its hardness. Hope blossomed

within me that with the power of the Honorable Forerunner, he would heal me.

Father Nicephorus applied a thousand and two poultices to me. What didn't he devise! Herbs, roots, leaves, fruits, pork fat, snails, heated bricks, various oils. But the abscess neither subsided nor softened. On the contrary, it worsened.

Then the elder decided to operate on me. He wanted to strike the evil at its root, which, as he said, was as large as a chickpea. He would therefore plunge the knife deep and, by removing the root which was the beginning of the evil, the entire abscess would soon disappear. I, however, feared the surgeon's boldness. An abscess that had not matured should not be operated on. Therefore, I refused the intervention. Thus, Father Nicephorus despaired of my cure, while I despaired of my life.

Completely disappointed by human help, I turned to the Mother of mercy, and persistently begged her with tears to become my physician and healer. "Look with your merciful eye and visit the affliction which I have," I lamented in a low voice.

Afterwards, I turned to those present and told them, "Take me to the chapel of the Theotokos of the Akathist, and leave me before her miraculous icon." Indeed, they carried me there. And while the priest chanted the Great Paraklesis for my sake, I wept continuously. Finally, I fell before the icon of the Panagia and, after wetting the ground with my tears, I pleaded fervently and said, "Do not leave me, Mother, to perish. Stop my misfortune. For you can do all things, being the Mother of God who is powerful in all things."

That was it! Immediately I felt strength within me, got up, and joyfully left the chapel. With the help of a brother and my staff, I climbed to my cell and finally slept through the whole night—I, who had spent so many nights sleepless from pain.

In the morning, I was calm. The abscess soon withered and disappeared. Since then, I feel indebted to the Theotokos and proclaim her miracle everywhere.

[24]

The Monk Hilarion

Moldavia is the name of the northern part of Romania, which united in 1918 with Transylvania and Wallachia, thus creating the modern state of Romania. Moldavia is famous for its ascetic monasteries, its caves carved into the rocks of Buzău, its strong religious traditions, and the ancestral piety of its inhabitants. There dominates Mount Ceahlău, the Romanian "Holy Mountain," which has thrived with its cells and sketes for four centuries.

In this country, at the foot of the Carpathian Mountains with their ancient forests, is built the Sihăstria Monastery, in an enchanting location with green hills, gardens, and an artificial pond with fish. The monastery was named Sihăstria because it is indeed very conducive to hesychasm (spiritual quietude). It began in the seventeenth century as a hesychastic center, and in 1655 it took the form of a monastery.

Here, in this monastery, lived and practiced asceticism the monk Hilarion Ionică (1854-1934), John in the world, from the community of Racova Bacău. Before coming to the monastery, he worked as a shipbuilder on the Bistritsa

River. There he experienced the following ordeal, which opened the way for him to the monastic life.

It was night in the wintertime. John had finished his work at the shipyard and was preparing to return home. Passing through the forest, he heard howls. They were wolves, and they soon attacked him. For two whole hours, he fought with them. His strength was exhausted. He realized he wouldn't make it and resorted to the powerful protection of the Theotokos, for whom he had special reverence since childhood. So, he knelt and cried out, "Most Holy Theotokos, if you grant me my life, I will leave everything and become a monk!"

Immediately, voices and bells were heard. It was a sleigh approaching rapidly. The frightened wolves fled, and John, now free, returned to his home.

Not much time passed, and John, faithful to his promise, abandoned the world and entered the community at Sihăstria Monastery. There in the monastery, after a year, he faced another trial. Melancholy overcame him, and he thought of leaving for another monastery. One night, sad as he was, he left his cell and went to the church to pray. At some point, he lifted his eyes and saw coming out of the icon of the Theotokos a woman in monastic attire. It was the Panagia herself! She approached him and asked, "Why are you weeping, brother John? Why are you troubled?"

"Well, I've grown weary here and want to leave this monastery."

"Why have you despaired in my house? Be at peace and do everything with love, and henceforth you will not experience despondency again."

Then the Theotokos returned again to the icon and disappeared. John was immediately freed from the temptation. Indeed, through his struggle, he became a model of humility and love, and was tonsured a monk with the name Hilarion.

Twenty years passed, when a third trial found him. One day, in the spring of 1933, he set out for the forest to cut wood. While working there, he injured his leg. The wound was serious and later developed gangrene. Father Hilarion again resorted to the Panagia: "Lady Theotokos, have mercy on me, do not abandon me!" he pleaded with tears.

At night, while praying, he saw a nun enter his cell. This nun resembled a doctor he knew.

"Why are you weeping?" she asked him.

"Lady doctor, I hurt my leg and I am in terrible pain. I understand that I will die, and I weep because I have not yet repented."

Then the nun looked at the leg, touched it with her hand, and said, "Do not weep anymore, Father Hilarion. Your leg is healed. You will live for another year, and then you will rest eternally."

The doctor left, and the elder fell asleep. In the morning, he rose healthy! Then he understood that the doctor was the Panagia herself. He immediately ran to the church and narrated the miracle to all the fathers. And in exactly one year, he commended his soul into the embrace of the Most Holy Theotokos.

[6]

The Blind Paralytic

Once, the monk Anthimus of Dionysiou Monastery visited a newly tonsured monk, who had fallen ill, in the monastery's hospital. To console him, he recounted a personal experience:

> My brother, set your hope in our Panagia, the great physician and protectress of monks. Listen

Dionysiou Monastery, Mount Athos

to an adventure of mine, so you may marvel at her mighty protection.

When I was your age, twenty-five years old and indeed newly tonsured, I fell gravely ill. I became like a corpse for a long time. I did not know what illness it was—rheumatism or something else—but I felt great weakness throughout my body. To walk, I used crutches. As if that weren't enough, my eyes also dimmed, and I could barely see in front of me.

Two doctors came and examined me. But they couldn't help me with anything. Moreover, as time passed, my condition worsened. Day and night I wept and said: "My Christ, what has befallen me!

Am I apparently the most sinful? A young monk, to find myself blind and paralyzed in the hospital, being served by the elders? Better that I die!"

Many brothers advised me to go out into the world, to be seen by better doctors. However, one brother, very pious and venerable, who loved me particularly, approached me and said, "Listen, my child. As you know, we have here in our monastery an old and historic icon, but above all miraculous, the Panagia of the Akathist Hymn. It is a gift from Emperor Alexios III Komnenos to the founder of our monastery. On its silver lining and the ancient wood, inscriptions survive, testifying that this was the icon which Patriarch Sergius carried around the walls of Constantinople and repelled the Persians and Avars in 626. And before this same icon, they subsequently chanted the Akathist Hymn (Salutations) for the first time, thanking the Theotokos for their salvation. Tradition relates that it is one of the seventy icons painted by the Evangelist Luke. Many times, indeed, it has gushed forth fragrant myrrh. Go, therefore, kneel before it and pray with fervent faith and tears, especially now that her feast day approaches. And she, being a compassionate Mother, will have mercy on you too, the suffering one."

These words gave me courage. They strengthened my faith, and I turned with all my soul to the Panagia, begging her with fervent tears.

When her feast day [of the Akathist Hymn] arrived, the fifth Saturday of Great Lent, I went to the church the evening before and kept vigil. I prayed much before her icon. Since I was tired, sleep overtook me right there.

Icon of the Virgin Mary of the Akathist,
Dionysiou Monastery, Mt. Athos, Greece.
Due to the flow of myrrh, the figures on the icon have become almost indistinguishable, but it continues to be a focal point of veneration.

Laudation to the Mother of God,
with the Akathist in 24 scenes,
collection of Mikhail De Buar (Elizavetin), Russia

And then, what was this! I saw the Panagia dressed all in gold, within a most brilliant light, shining with radiance and glory. She stood two cubits high from the ground and looked at me with a serene gaze. Then she opened her honey-sweet mouth and said to me, "Why are you weeping, my child Anthimus?"

"How can I not weep, my Panagia? Don't You see my wretched state, how I have ended up?"

"Do not weep, but attend to your salvation."

She told me this, blessed me, and ascended.

Immediately I awoke. I rubbed my eyes and saw the oil lamps lit. I summoned the courage to stand up, and found that I walked with ease. Immediately I understood! The Panagia had performed her miracle and had completely healed me. Oh, what joy I felt! How many tears of thanksgiving I shed! How many hymns I sang cannot be described!

Soon the sacristan opened the church. He saw me walking and could not believe his eyes. One by one, all the fathers approached me. And when they saw me healthy, they glorified the Lord and His all-pure Mother from the depths of their souls for her infinite love.

[24]

The Nun Hermione

Hermina had not yet completed a year of marriage when the dreaded illness befell her. A doctor herself, an honors graduate with a career, she knew very well what cancer meant. The pain, small at first, grew continually until it confined her to bed. Her husband, Errikos, instead of comforting her, grumbled heavily, "Confound it all! What misfortune has befallen me!"

"Have patience and hope, my son," Hermina's grandmother advised him. "God is great."

"If He is great, why does He condescend to pick on us little ones?" he protested.

The illness dragged on. Errikos couldn't bear to see his partner in such a state, nor did he offer her any encouragement. Hermina was completely orphaned. Her only support was her good grandmother. Thanks to her, she had taken the good path and had become a modest, serious, and pious character.

"My grandmother, how much I trouble you now when I should be helping you!"

"Don't worry, my dear girl. Who knows? Our Panagia also performs miracles. Morning and night, I beg her with tears to grant you health. You pray to her too."

She was admitted to the hospital, as her condition was constantly deteriorating.

"At the current stage of the illness, there is no hope," the doctors diagnosed, withdrawing silently from the sick woman's bed.

"Grandmother," Hermina begged one day, "go to the hospital chaplain to say a Paraklesis to the Panagia for me. Then I want him to come and hear my confession so I can receive Communion."

The grandmother fulfilled her wish. She even brought her an expressive icon of the Lady of Great Grace and told her, "Turn, my daughter, to look at her, talk to her, and take courage."

One evening, the grandmother was walking down the hospital corridor. Suddenly, she saw before her a very sweet female figure, dressed in the pristine white uniform of a head nurse.

She was surprised. This wasn't one of those she knew.

"I see you for the first time, head nurse," she remarked. "Will you be here with us now? It's an honor for us."

The stranger replied, "I am the Panagia. I heard your prayers and came to help you. Tomorrow morning, Hermina will be well. Only let her devote herself more to my Son and God." Saying this, she vanished.

The elderly woman stood petrified. Everything spun before her. It took effort for her to regain her balance. Then she hastened her steps towards her granddaughter. She found her cheerful too.

"My Hermina, this and this happened to me."

"Yes, grandmother, the All-Pure One came to me too. She caressed my head and gave me courage. I don't hurt anymore. I feel light."

During their morning visit, the doctors beheld an inexplicable sight: the patient was sitting dressed on a chair. As soon as she saw them, she stood up cheerfully to greet them.

"Strange!" they said among themselves. "This is surely a cure by autosuggestion. It seems a psychological or parapsychological movement has occurred."

"Gentlemen colleagues!" Hermina then took the floor. "I inform you and, as a doctor, I assure you that none of what you say is happening. My cure is due exclusively to the Most Holy Theotokos."

Errikos also heard the news. But he had his doubts. "Surely this is a temporary improvement," he observed. "These illnesses often return with metastases. I have no confidence."

"But nothing physiological happened here. A miracle occurred!" explained the healed woman.

"I don't believe in miracles. The first scare is enough for me."

"And then what will happen?"

"Take responsibility for your life on your own."

Thus he spoke and left heavily.

Hermina felt dizzy. It was something unexpected. But immediately she remembered the Panagia's advice "to devote herself more to her Son and God."

"Ah, yes, my Christ, my Panagia!" she exclaimed. "Only Your love remains steadfast. That is what I need. That will fulfill me."

So she left her hometown of Patras, traveling far away to a renowned monastery, and there—as Sister Hermione—she dedicated and devoted herself wholeheartedly to her bridegroom Christ.

[10]

The Teacher

Maria Kalogerou, a young teacher from Kimolos, suffered from severe neurasthenia, which eventually developed into a state approaching madness. She was hospitalized for a considerable time in a clinic in Athens, but showed no improvement.

Desperate, her brother and mother made a vow for her to the Evangelistria of Tinos, where they arrived via the steamship "Samos."

As soon as they disembarked, the mother and brother wanted to lead her to the church of the Theotokos. She, however, resisted for fear they would tie her up and imprison her. They therefore stayed in a hotel, and in the evening went out for a walk.

At some point, the sick woman felt an irresistible force drawing her towards the church, and she asked to be taken there. The church was closed at that hour. However, not wanting to disappoint her, they proceeded into the churchyard, climbed the marble steps, and stood before the closed church door.

Maria's brother glanced through the glass towards the sanctuary, then turned and said, "We are lucky! Inside the church, there is a nun, and she will come to open for us." The mother approached the glass and also saw a tall woman dressed in black. She turned to the sick woman, saw her gazing ecstatically and moving towards the entrance, as if seeing something supernatural.

Suddenly, the woman in black disappeared, while at the same time a loud noise was heard from inside the church. The custodian was notified, and subsequently the head priest and the president of the foundation. They carefully searched the church and confirmed that no one was inside. At the same time, however, they confirmed that the sick woman had recovered and felt herself to be healthy.

The miracle quickly spread throughout the island, and people began flocking to the church starting that very night. The bells rang joyfully, and an extraordinary doxology was chanted. The emotion of the faithful peaked, however, when the healed teacher came forward and received the Immaculate Mysteries.

[35]

Resurrection from the Dead

Anastasius, a three-year-old boy, was the sole consolation of his mother Sophia, ever since her husband abandoned her. Now, however, it was the second day that Anastasios lay dead, ravaged by the claws of death after an unequal struggle.

Her inexhaustible maternal love had offered all it could. She now looks at his pale face and cannot believe her eyes. She caressed the cold body, touched the stiff hands, and a heart-wrenching cry escaped her: "My Panagia, how can I believe it?"

With eyes bloodshot from crying and sleeplessness, she wandered like a ghost through the empty house, while her memory flitted to strange and distant worlds. She imagined a crowd of people passing before her. Among them, she distinguished her deceased parents, holding her unfortunate child by the hand. She ran to snatch him from their hands, but it was a futile effort.

When she came to, she again saw the harsh reality. "My Panagia, full of grace," she pleaded, "give me back my Tasos! See, I beg you kneeling before your miraculous icon!"

Dusk gave way to night, and when dawn began to break, something unexpected happened: the lips of the dead child began to turn pink; the lifeless body took breath.

The mother opened her eyes wide to convince herself she wasn't deceived. But the faint voice of Anastasius better convinced her of his resurrection. The Most Gracious Lady had performed her miracle.

Years passed. Sophia Mandili from Avlonari, Euboea, the now happy mother, who had emigrated to Edmonton, Canada, wrote in a letter to the holy foundation of Evangelistria, Tinos:

> "March 15, 1938.
>
> "I am sending you a photograph of myself and my child. The Panagia resurrected him for me when he was three years old and had been dead for three days. Her grace, whom I begged like one mad with pain, brought him back to life for me. Now I send you his photograph, so you can see him as a fine young man."

In another letter, she notes:

> "I had hoped to come and venerate her icon and stay near her forever. But it was not possible for me.

The Most Gracious Lady, the shelter and support of the world—when I pray to her, I feel her beside me, my consolation. And as long as I am alive, her name will never leave my lips."

[35]

The Blasphemer

In 1915, the Athenian press published accounts of various miracles performed by the icon of the Most Gracious Lady (Panagia of Tinos), which had been transferred to Athens. The transfer of the holy icon had taken place for the purpose of healing the gravely ill King Constantine, who indeed was miraculously cured.

In the morning newspaper "Astrapi," the following miracle is recorded, as narrated by the merchant Dimitrios Bournias, who maintained a shop at 36 Agiou Markou Street:

> Last Wednesday, July 8, 1915, I was hosting a close friend of mine at my home. At noon, while we were eating, I said to him, "Glory to God! The Most Gracious Lady of Tinos performed her miracle, and the king was saved."
>
> He then interrupted me and uttered disrespectfully, "Oh, never mind that old piece of wood they brought." However, he had not finished the phrase when he abruptly clutched his throat as if he had swallowed a burning coal. At the same moment, he felt shortness of breath, lost his speech, while his eyes looked terrified and pleading. We all then got up to help him, to bring him water, but he refused everything.
>
> Suddenly, an inspiration came to me. I ran to the iconostasis in the next room, took an icon of the

Panagia, and brought it to him. As soon as he saw it, he spontaneously knelt, stretched out his hands, and kissed it with reverence.

At the same moment, he felt healed, and with tears in his eyes, he said, “God punished me because I blasphemed. But the Most Gracious Lady performed her miracle for me too.”

[35]

Copy of the icon Panagia of Tinos

PART III

BENEFICIAL VISIONS

St. Catherine the Great Martyr (17th century icon)
by Victor of Crete

Saint Catherine

The great martyr Catherine, daughter of Constas, the ruler of Alexandria, was martyred for Christ in the early fourth century, during the reign of Maximinus.

Before becoming a Christian, many senators sought her hand in marriage due to her rare wisdom and beauty. Her mother, a secret Christian because of the emperor's terrible persecution, as well as other relatives, advised her to marry so that her father's authority would not fall into foreign hands.

She, however, disagreed. Since her relatives insisted, she told them, "I accept to marry, but I desire my husband to be superior to me in noble birth, beauty, wealth, and wisdom."

Despite all their searches, no one was found who possessed all four of these gifts to a superior degree than the saint.

Outside the city lived a holy ascetic in hiding, who was her mother's spiritual father. She led Catherine to him so he could solve their problem.

The ascetic, upon seeing the prudent young woman and hearing her knowledgeable words, thought to draw her to Christ.

"I know a marvelous Man," he told her, "Who greatly surpasses you in all the gifts you mentioned, and in countless others. The radiance of His beauty outshines the sun. His wisdom governs all perceptible and intelligible creations. His wealth is distributed throughout the world but constantly increases. Finally, His nobility is ineffable and incomprehensible."

Catherine, captivated by what she heard, asked, "This Man Whom you praise so highly, who is His father?"

"He has no earthly father. But He was born supernaturally from a Most Holy Virgin."

"Could I see Him?"

"If you do what I tell you, you will be worthy to see Him."

"I see you are a knowledgeable man, therefore I am ready to do whatever you command me."

Then the spiritual father took an icon of the Theotokos holding the Infant Christ, offered it to the young woman, and told her, "This is the ever-virgin Mother of that Man with the many gifts. Take it home, pray before it all night, and ask her to show you her Son. I hope that if you pray with faith, she will fulfill your request."

Catherine took the holy icon, went to her palace, shut herself in her room at night, and began to pray. At some point, from exhaustion, she fell asleep. She then saw in her sleep the Theotokos, as she was depicted in the icon with the Divine Infant. The Lord, however, had His face turned away.

Catherine changed position so she could see it, but the Lord turned away from her again. This was repeated a third time, whereupon she heard the Panagia saying to Him, "Look, my Child, at Your servant Catherine, who surpasses all the young women of the world in wealth, wisdom, and nobility!"

The Lord then remarked, "No, Mother! As long as she remains in the delusion of idols, she is illiterate, poor, and despised. Therefore, I cannot look upon her."

"I beg you, my Child, do not despise Your creation. Tell her what she must do to enjoy Your glory and behold Your face."

"Let her go to the elder who gave her the icon, and let her do whatever he advises her."

Catherine awoke full of wonder. Early in the morning, she went to the elder, narrated with tears what she had seen and heard, and asked him what to do to fulfill her desire. He then catechized her in the mysteries of the true Faith. In a short time, Catherine was instructed with all accuracy. And she did not learn the Christian Faith only in theory, but believed with all her heart and finally received holy baptism. Afterwards, the elder instructed her to pray to the Theotokos, so that she might appear to her again.

Now Catherine, clothed in the God-woven garment of holy baptism and purified by fasting, prayed in her room until late at night. At some point when she fell asleep, she again saw the Divine Infant in the embrace of the Virgin.

"How do You see the young woman now?" the Panagia asked the Lord.

"Yes, now she has become bright and glorious, rich and all-wise, noble and full of grace. I regard her so highly that I accept her as My bride."

Catherine, hearing the Lord's words, knelt tearfully. "I am not worthy, Master, to reign with you. Grant me the favor to be numbered among your servants."

Then the Lady Theotokos took the young woman's right hand and pleaded, "Grant her, Lord, the ring of betrothal, so You may betroth her and deem her worthy to reign with You."

Immediately, Jesus Christ gave her a most beautiful ring and told her, "Behold! From today you are My bride. Guard this agreement carefully and never associate with an earthly bridegroom."

As soon as Catherine awoke, she indeed saw a ring on her right hand. And immediately her heart was captivated by the divine love of the Lord Christ.

[41]

Saint Cyril of Alexandria

Saint Cyril, Patriarch of Alexandria (+444), was the bold opponent of Nestorius and champion of the title "Theotokos" for the Ever-Virgin Mary. At the Third Ecumenical Council in 431, he fought with boldness for the Mother of God. His struggles for the Mother of the Lord earned her special favor for him, as the following incident reveals.

In a suburb of Chalcedon, at Drys, a robber council was convened, which condemned Saint John Chrysostom in absentia. Saint Cyril, out of ignorance and not malice, adopted the decisions of the council and reached the point of not wanting to commemorate the saint's name in the diptychs, along with the names of the other patriarchs.

However, he was well-intentioned, and when the appropriate recommendations were made to him, he examined matters more closely, recognized his error, and corrected his stance. Contributing to this change was the following dream:

It seemed to him that he was in a most beautiful place and experienced an ineffable joy. He saw there the patriarchs Abraham, Isaac, and Jacob, as well as other men of the Old and New Testaments. He also saw a very bright and magnificent church, from which heavenly psalmody was heard. He proceeded into the church and beheld the Most Holy Theotokos, surrounded by a multitude of holy angels, shining with ineffable glory. Near the Mother of God stood Saint John Chrysostom with great honor and many attendants, holding the book of his teachings in his hands.

Saint Cyril went forward to venerate the Most Holy Theotokos. Saint John, however, interposed himself and not only prevented him but also wanted to cast him out. Terrified, he wondered why Saint Chrysostom could be so angry with him. Then the Panagia intervened and said, "Forgive him, John, and do not cast him out. Whatever he has said against you, he said not out of malice, but out of ignorance."

St. Cyril of Alexandria
(14th century fresco)
King's Church, Monastery
Studenica, Serbia

"No, I do not forgive him," the saint pretended to say angrily.

"Forgive him for my love," the Panagia insisted, "because he fought much for my honor, refuted Nestorius, and proclaimed me as Theotokos."

Immediately, he calmed down, embraced his former opponent, and kissed him with love.

From then on, Saint Cyril's esteem for Saint John was boundless. Saint Cyril fought on the patriarchal throne of Alexandria for thirty-two years. And when he was commending his holy soul, the Panagia did not forget him. She came to him and attended him with care, just as he had served her faithfully in his life and fought for her honor.

[28]

Saint Romanus the Melodist

Saint Romanus, although a tested laborer of virtue, was nevertheless completely unmusical and cacophonous. So much so, that he was often mocked and ridiculed.

His homeland was Emesa in Syria, and he had served as a deacon in Beirut. In 496, during the reign of Emperor Anastasius I, he came to Constantinople. Here he was fond of frequenting and keeping vigil in the church of the Panagia of Blachernae, but even more so in the church of the Theotokos at Kyros, where he spent day and night in vigils and prayers.

In this church, there was an icon of the Theotokos that performed countless miracles. Before this icon, the deacon fell down and begged her to grant him the gift of melody.

One Christmas night, the saint was attending the vigil in the church. During the sixth ode, while he was near the ambo, sleep overtook him for a moment. He then saw the Theotokos holding a kontakion scroll, a paper rolled cylindrically, and she said to him, "Take and eat it." He indeed took it, and it seemed to him that he swallowed it. From that moment, he received the desired gift. He awoke immediately, ascended the ambo, and began to chant the troparion, "Today the Virgin gives birth to the Transcendent One…"

Saint Romanus composed over a thousand kontakia regarding the feasts of the Lord, the Theotokos, and the commemorations of saints.

[41]

St. Romanus the Melodist (13th century fresco)
Theotokos Church, Monastery Studenica, Serbia

The Two Discourses of Nestorius

Abba Kyriakos (fifth-sixth century) was a presbyter in the Lavra of Kalamon, near the Jordan River. He once narrated the following:

> One night, I saw in my sleep a woman dressed in purple, with a modest appearance, and two venerable and reverend men standing outside my cell. I understood that the woman was the Most Holy Theotokos herself, while of the men, one was Saint John the Theologian and the other the Honorable Forerunner.
>
> I came out of my cell and begged them to come inside to bless it. The Theotokos, however, refused. I insisted for a long time, begging her, whereupon she replied sternly, "You have my enemy in your cell, and how do you want me to enter?" Upon saying this, she departed.
>
> When I awoke, I began to think, distressed, lest I had sinned in thought against her. There was no one else in my cell but me. For a long time, I examined myself but found no fault in anything against her.
>
> Then I got up, very saddened, and took a book to read, to dispel my sorrow with reading. The book was by Saint Hesychios, presbyter of Jerusalem. As I was leafing through it, I found towards the end two discourses by the impious Nestorius. I immediately understood that this was the enemy of the Theotokos. I then got up and returned it to the one who had given it to me, saying, "Take your book, brother, for I was harmed more than I benefited."
>
> When I explained the events to him, he zealously cut out the two discourses of Nestorius and threw

them into the fire, saying, "The enemy of the Most Holy Theotokos and Ever-Virgin Mary shall not remain in my cell."

[17]

The Heretical Patrician Woman

A certain patrician woman named Cosmiana (sixth century) came one night to venerate the Holy Sepulchre in Jerusalem. As she approached, the Lady Theotokos appeared to her with other women and said to her, "You are not permitted to enter here, for you are not one of us."

She said this because Cosmiana belonged to the heresy of Severus. Cosmiana, however, insisted and begged to be allowed entry. Then the Theotokos replied, "It is impossible for you to enter here unless you first come into mystical communion with us."

Then the patrician woman understood that her entry was hindered because she was a heretic, and that unless she converted to the Orthodox Church, she would not venerate the Holy Sepulchre.

And so she did. First, she abandoned the heresy of Severus. Then, repentant, she called the deacon and received the Immaculate Mysteries. Then she proceeded unhindered and venerated the life-giving tomb of Christ the Savior.

[17]

Saint John Koukouzelis

Saint John Koukouzelis, surnamed "the angel-voiced" for his truly angelic voice, was born in Dyrrhachium in 1270, during the reign of the Komnenoi. Because of his exceptional voice, he was recruited into a royal music school. He was also excellent in character, for which the king loved him exceedingly, as did all the nobles. He himself, however, fearing that transient glory might deprive him of heavenly exultation, planned to depart from the world.

Once, the abbot of the Lavra of Athos visited the king on necessary business. The sight of the abbot and his propriety fanned the desire for the angelic life in the young man's heart. He therefore disregarded the royal favor, exchanged his silk clothes for haircloth, took a staff, and set out for the Lavra.

The gatekeeper of the monastery asked him, "What do you seek, and what art do you know?"

John, hiding his true art lest the king discover him, replied, "I am a shepherd and desire to become a monk."

The abbot received him, tested him for a short time, and after tonsuring him a monk, sent him to the mountain to graze goats. Thus, the saint fulfilled his desire and, while performing his service, prayed at the same time undisturbed in his beloved quietude.

One day, he was grazing the goats on a cape. He looked right and left, made sure no one was there, and began to chant a hymn with exceeding art and compunction. An ascetic nearby heard the heavenly melody and came out of his cave, astonished. He then saw an exquisite sight: the goats had stopped grazing and were watching the excellent chanter. This event soon came to the abbot's knowledge. From then on, the saint utilized his rare gift, chanting in the right choir of the Lavra's katholikon (main church).

It was the Saturday of the Akathist Hymn, and Koukouzelis, after diligently chanting the idiomela and the canon of the Theotokos, fell asleep for a little while from fatigue, standing in his stall. He then saw before him the Most Holy Theotokos and heard her sweet voice saying, "Rejoice,

Saint John Koukouzelis

Panagia Koukouzelissa

John, my child. Chant to me, and I will not abandon you." Upon saying this, she gave him a gold coin.

The saint awoke immediately and saw with joy the florin in his right hand. He thanked the Theotokos for her favor and handed it over to the church. This coin possessed miraculous power and performed great wonders.

From then on, Saint John was never absent from the right choir, chanting with zeal and glorifying the Lord and His Mother. From much labor and prolonged standing, his leg rotted and discharged a foul-smelling substance. The Panagia, however, did not abandon him. She appeared again and said to him, "From now on, you will be healthy." Immediately, the saint was healed and remained healthy until the end of his life. He even foresaw his death, asked forgiveness from all the brothers, and fell asleep in holiness on October 1.

[41]

The Protection of the Theotokos

The feast of the Holy Protection (Skepi) of the Theotokos (October 1 and, later, October 28) draws its subject matter from the life of Saint Andrew, the Fool-for-Christ. The appearance of the Theotokos to the saint was the occasion for the establishment of this feast.

The incident occurred in the south side of the church of Blachernae, in the chapel of the Holy Soros (Reliquary), where the robe, veil, and part of the belt of the Theotokos were kept. In this chapel, an all-night vigil was once being held. Saint Andrew also went there to pray with his disciple, Saint Epiphanios.

About 10 p.m. the saint saw the Theotokos advancing from the royal gates towards the holy sanctuary. She appeared very tall and had a splendid honor guard of saints

The Protection of the Mother of God (1399) Zverin Monastery, Russia

dressed in white. Among them, the Honorable Forerunner and John the Theologian stood out, walking to her right and left. Of those dressed in white, some preceded and others followed, chanting hymns and spiritual songs.

When they approached the ambo, Saint Andrew said to Epiphanios, "Do you see, my child, the Lady and Mistress of the world?"

"Yes, venerable father," replied the young man.

The Theotokos at that moment knelt and prayed for a long time. She beseeched her Son for the salvation of the world and wet her face with tears. Afterwards, she entered the holy sanctuary and prayed for the faithful who were keeping vigil.

When she finished her prayer, with a graceful and modest movement, she removed from her immaculate head the radiant maphorion (veil), and spread it like a protection with her all-holy hands over the congregation. Both St. Andrew and St. Epiphanius saw it thus spread for a long time, emitting divine glory. As long as the Theotokos was visible there, the holy maphorion was also seen scattering its grace. When she began to ascend to heaven, it too began to contract little by little and disappear.

[27]

Saint Seraphim of Sarov

From the host of Russian saints, Saint Seraphim of Sarov nourished a special love for the Panagia. But the Mother of God also enveloped him with particular favor, as her many appearances to him prove.

The following vision of the saint is the most impressive. It is narrated by the nun Eupraxia of Diveyevo, because she too was deemed worthy to enjoy it with the saint:

> Early in the morning of March 25, 1831, a loud noise was heard, followed by a harmonious hymn. The door of the room opened on its own, and light and fragrance spread everywhere. Starets [Elder] Seraphim was kneeling with his hands raised. I was trembling. Suddenly, he rose and told me, "Do not be afraid, my child. Behold, our Lady, the Most Holy Theotokos, is coming to us!"
>
> Indeed, two angels went ahead holding flowering branches. They were followed by the Honorable Forerunner and Saint John the Theologian, while

behind them the Panagia made her appearance with twelve virgin martyrs.

The Theotokos, wearing a radiant mantle and a magnificent crown, approached me while I lay prostrate on the ground. She touched me and deigned to say to me, "Rise, sister, and do not be afraid. With me have come virgins like you." I did not understand how I got up. The queen repeated, "Do not be afraid. We have come to visit you."

Father Seraphim, standing before the Panagia, spoke with her with great intimacy. The Theotokos told him many things. Although I participated in the vision, I could not hear what they were saying. I only heard the following:

"Do not abandon my virgins of Diveyevo."

"O Lady! I gather them, but I cannot guide them alone."

"I will help you in everything. You will teach them obedience. If they keep it, they will be with you and near me. Otherwise, they will lose the place I am preparing for them among these virgins here. Neither such a place nor such a crown will they enjoy. Whoever offends them will be punished by me. And whoever serves them for the love of Christ will find mercy before Him."

Then the Panagia turned to me. She told me, "Look at these virgins and their crowns. Some left earthly kingdoms and riches for the heavenly kingdom. All loved voluntary poverty, loved only the Lord, and that is why you see how much glory and honor they were deemed worthy of. Just as the ancient martyrs suffered, so do the present ones suffer. Only those suffered openly, while today they

Painting of St. Seraphim of Sarov.
Saint Seraphim is said to have allowed this portrait only with the greatest reluctance.

suffer secretly, with sorrow of heart. But their reward will be the same."

Then, turning to the starets, the Theotokos blessed him and said to him, "Soon, my beloved, you will be with us!"

The saint exchanged greetings with her, as well as with all the saints. One of them turned and told me, "You were deemed worthy of this vision thanks to the prayers of Fathers Seraphim, Mark, Nazary, and Pachomios."

Suddenly, everything vanished. The vision, which had lasted less than an hour, ended. It was the twelfth that Saint Seraphim was deemed worthy to enjoy in his earthly life.

[36]

Answer to Doubts

The Monastery of Saint Paul dominates majestically and imposingly at the foothills of Athos. The year 1839 was very important for the monastery because its transformation took place from an idiorrhythmic to a cenobitic way of life. Unrest and scandals followed.

A certain monk doubted whether such an abrupt transformation was pleasing to God. Furthermore, he did not look favorably upon the other monks generously giving alms to the poor, at a time when the monastery had great needs and many debts.

The Panagia, however, wished to dispel his doubts and inform him that the establishment of the coenobium was God's will and that she herself provides for the needs of the monastery and the monks.

Not much time passed before this brother fell ill in bed. He then fell into an ecstasy and saw Satan raging and

Monastery of Saint Paul, Mount Athos

gnashing his teeth. The reason was the cenobitic conversion of the monastery and his envy regarding the spiritual salvation of its monks. So, he set traps and snares, prepared scandals and disturbances, to torment the abbot and the monks and thus dissolve the coenobium.

On December 31, 1844, the day of the consecration of the monastery's katholikon, the same monk was again gravely ill. And while he was in his bed, he saw in an ecstasy that he was present at the celebration. But he also saw something astounding: a most modest Virgin sitting on the sacred synthronon (bishop's throne) within the holy sanctuary. She held in her embrace an Infant Who shone brighter than the sun and had in His hands a royal scepter.

At times, she would come out of the holy sanctuary and stand sometimes in the right and sometimes in the left choir, to regulate the chanters and strengthen the deacons. Other times, she would walk around the church, observing with satisfaction the columns and their pedestals, and then she would strengthen them so that they would remain forever stable. At other times, within the sanctuary, she herself, along with the bishop and the priests, prepared the myrrh and mixtures for the consecration. She presided and directed everything within her house.

A month before the monastery's feast day, the aforementioned monk was again ill in his cell. He then fell into ecstasy for the third time and saw himself in the church attending the vigil. In the apse of the holy sanctuary, on the synthronon, the Virgin was again seated with the Divine Infant in her embrace, adorned with her purple maphorion, as she is depicted in iconography. At some point, she stood up, took off her radiant maphorion, left it on the holy synthronon, and after preparing her hands for service, she went out into the main church. There she began to bless the priests and deacons, to coordinate the chanters, the canonarchs, and the ecclesiarchs, to give orders for everything. During the litany, she went outside the church, preceded all those who took part in it, chanted, and rejoiced with them.

During the Divine Liturgy, she spent most of the time in the holy sanctuary with the bishop and the priests. Later, at the refectory, she supervised the deacons who were serving the food and served alongside them. Everywhere she served with diligence and blessed.

When the meal ended and the monks came out, the Virgin also came out and went to the monastery gate. There sat the poor and beggars waiting for alms. The Lady showed them mercy and blessed them. And when she approached the virtuous, she had a cheerful countenance, while towards the slothful and negligent, she appeared serious and stern.

Meanwhile, the refectory attendants and cooks sat down to eat. Among them, the monk who was seeing the vision saw himself. But, behold, the Lady Theotokos came to serve them too with love. Only then did he understand that the woman he was seeing was the Panagia herself. He immediately rose, knelt before her, venerated her, and said, "Lady Theotokos, it is not for you to serve me, but for me to serve you. It is my duty, your unworthy servant."

And saying this, he took a plate, which by a nod from the Theotokos perhaps appeared there, put two baked fish in it, and approached her.

"Lady," he pleaded, "sit with me to eat."

"I do not eat such food, nor does my Son," she replied. "However, because I was invited to this feast, I strengthened those who labored and helped them in attending to the guests, for I learned from my Son to glorify those who glorify me, to honor those who honor me, and to offer them whatever they ask of me through their prayers."

Thus spoke the Theotokos, admonishing the monk, and after raising her immaculate hands, she prayed and blessed the monastery, the abbot, and the monks. Then a transcendent light poured forth and bathed them all. Immediately, the Lady ascended to heaven and vanished, leaving the monk in a state of divine alteration, joy, and gladness.

[25]

The Vision of the Hesychast

The noetic prayer, the Jesus Prayer, is the central theme of the book "Neptic Theory" [entitled *The Watchful Mind* in English]. Its author, the anonymous hesychast, the self-proclaimed "Desperate One," reveals his experiences and offers his expertise to the reader as a guide for mastering noetic prayer.

This practical teacher presents with naturalness and particular sweetness his appearances and conversations with the Lord, the Most Holy Theotokos, and the holy angels, often, out of modesty, attributing them to another person in his own stead. Such is the vision that follows narrated by the hesychast:

> A certain monk fell into ecstasy while praying and saw a multitude of demons, like the sand of the sea. They resembled soldiers and rushed against him with great fury, seeking to destroy him.
>
> Frightened, he ran to take refuge in the church. Entering, he saw the Lord and the Theotokos in their icons as if alive and with royal glory. The face of the Lord had an ineffable beauty and shone brighter than the Sun. Therefore, the brother could not look again. However, he venerated and kissed His right hand with fear and joy.

Then he approached the icon of the Panagia. He venerated, kissed her virginal hand, and dared to look at her face. In her holy embrace, he saw the Divine Infant seated as if on a cherubic throne. And this divine complex was as harmonious as the beauty and fragrance in a rose.

The Theotokos looked at the brother with such gentleness that he took courage and asked her, "My Panagia! My sweet Panagia, and Mother of my Jesus! How will I escape from the demons that hunt me?"

And the Lady Theotokos, the salvation of those who trust in her, replied, "By the name of my Son and by my own name, you will conquer and annihilate the demons."

The monk bowed deeply, came out of the church, and cried out from his heart, "Lord Jesus Christ, Son of God, have mercy on me! Theotokos Virgin, rejoice, Mary full of grace!" Immediately the powerless demons vanished from before him.

[4]

Papa Joachim Spetsieris

In the village of Kontogourata in Cephalonia, Father Joachim first saw the light of day in 1858. His grandfather, also a priest, foretold that the child would one day be ordained. At his baptism, he was named John, and from then on, his parents Gerasimos and Diamantoula, as well as all their acquaintances, called him Papa John.

In 1861, at the age of three, John fell gravely ill and was in danger of dying. His parents immediately vowed him [to be dedicated] to Panagia Drapaniotissa. They went to her

Hieromonk Joachim Spetsieris

holy church, knelt before the miraculous icon, and laid the unconscious infant there.

"O Lady," they prayed, "grant health to our child. And we vow to you, when he becomes twelve years old, to bring him here, dress him in monastic robes, and dedicate him to you." Immediately, the death rattle and fever subsided, and when they reached home, the little one was completely healthy.

John, from the age of five, had expressed a desire for monastic life. His parents, however, did not fulfill their vow, so the little one fell ill again and many times approached death. Despite all this, they continued to strongly oppose his desire for monastic life, resulting in frequent episodes at home.

One evening, heartbroken after a fierce attack from his father and uncle, John was monologuing and begging to die. All night he wept and sought the protection of the Theotokos. At some point, while kneeling, he heard in the depths of his heart the voice saying, "Holy Mountain," and immediately the desire to become a monk on Athos flared within him.

After many adventures, he set out for the Mountain at the age of nineteen. He traveled by steamship to Thessaloniki, rented an animal for a while, and finally, journeying through the forests, reached his destination.

He chose New Skete and joined the community in the cell of the Holy Unmercenaries, where, as a novice, he undertook all the heavy tasks. After a year of probation, he was tonsured

New Skete, Athos, seen from above

a monk and received the name Joachim. The excessive labors soon undermined his health and made him consumptive.

Illness was not his only temptation. He was greatly tormented by thoughts leading to despair. “O Lady,” he pleaded, “I want to die so as not to be a burden to others with my illness.”

And the Lady was not slow to answer. He recounted the following:

> One morning, after finishing the kneading, I went to my cell to rest. I was experiencing mental anguish and was begging the Theotokos to let me die. Suddenly, abundant light shone before me.
>
> “My Panagia!” I cried out, terrified. At the same time, I saw the Most Holy Theotokos in that light, while radiance emanated from her face and garments. As I looked at her, I suddenly found myself in the air, to her right, whereupon she extended her hand and said to me, “Do you see?”

> I turned my gaze thither and saw my body supine on the ground. From my mouth came forth two lilies, on each leaf of which were written in golden letters the words: "Most Holy Theotokos."
>
> "One lily," continued the Theotokos, "is of the soul and the other of the body. Whoever has his hope in me fears neither in this life nor in the next."
>
> Immediately the Panagia disappeared, and with her the thoughts that tormented me. My heart filled with joy and my eyes with tears. At the same time, the desire was born within me to go to the Holy Land, to stay and find peace there.
>
> The days passed without thoughts, but the pain in his chest and the hemoptysis continued.
>
> I resorted again to the Theotokos and sought her maternal intervention. One night she appeared in my sleep and, showing me Jerusalem, told me, 'Go to this city, and you will find rest.'

The young monk's desire soon became a reality. With the blessing of his elder, he went to Jerusalem and joined the community at the Monastery of Saint Savvas. Later he was transferred to the metochion (dependency) of the Holy Sepulchre in Athens, where he studied at the Rizareios School and then at the Theological School. As a preacher thereafter, he offered his services in various metropolises.

When he was serving in Chalkida, the head priest of the Greek community in Marseilles happened to die. Father Joachim submitted his candidacy but failed by one vote.

The protection of the Theotokos followed him and protected him everywhere, as is also evident from the following incident:

> The news of the failure saddened me, and confessing to my protectress Theotokos, I said with complaint, "Lady, I sought this position because I

> was entrusted to protect my two orphaned young relatives, Konstantinos and Vasilikoula. What will I do now?"
>
> Upon saying this, a light sleep overtook me. I then saw myself on a very high tower. My room was at its top, while at its base, the waves of an endless sea crashed with a roar.
>
> I was at a loss and, not knowing what to do, I rushed to jump from the window into the sea. However, I felt fear and terror, while at the same time a hand grabbed me by the clothes and dragged me violently backward. I turned immediately and saw the Lady Theotokos holding me and saying, "Do you want me to let you fall into this sea? Don't you see the waves?"
>
> With these words, I awoke and did not take long to understand their meaning. Indeed, high offices hide great dangers.

However, the titles and his life in the world did not affect the humble elder. His zeal for monasticism and nostalgia for the Holy Mountain always possessed him. That is why he returned in 1925, permanently this time, to his kalyvi in New Skete.

Until the end of his life, he maintained his undiminished reverence for the Theotokos, combined with intimacy and simplicity. When he wanted to do something, he always asked her. He did nothing without her blessing. Once he said charmingly to his subordinate, "I will leave today. I asked our dear Panagia, and she told me to leave."

Another time he also said, "Make coffee, Theophylaktos, for us to drink with the blessing of our dear Panagia."

"Elder, why are you crying?" his subordinate asked him.

"Well, my child, I remembered our dear Panagia."

And when the time for the eternal journey was approaching (in 1943), he would say the Salutations to the Panagia even in his sleep.

[19]

The White Bread

The venerable hieromonk Father Tychon (1884-1968), Russian by origin, practiced asceticism for sixty years on Athos. He had the habit, out of his great piety towards the Panagia, to read the Salutations to the Theotokos many times a day while weeping. A miracle of the Panagia was the reason for Father Tychon to decide on his monastic dedication.

Papa Tychon

In Siberia, where he was from, they had much wheat and their bread was white. When at a young age he was touring the Russian monasteries, he once arrived in Moscow. There they ate black bread, which he was not used to, and for this reason, he could not eat it. Thus he remained for some days fasting.

Passing once outside an oven, he saw a woman offering him a loaf of bread, dazzlingly white and hot. He had no money to pay for it. However, he entered the shop to find the woman and thank her.

"Where is the woman who gave me the bread?" he asked the baker.

"No woman came out of my shop," he replied. "Besides, we do not have white bread here."

The young man looked at the white, steaming bread he was holding in his hands, and his eyes welled up with emotion. Then he received the inner knowledge that this gift was from the Panagia. They both thanked the Theotokos, and the baker took a little of the bread as a blessing. With this bread, Father Tychon was nourished throughout his entire pilgrimage tour. After this miracle, he decided to dedicate himself to God and become a monk.

[32]

Elder Gelasius

Elder Gelasius first saw the light of day in Phocaea of Asia Minor. From his birth in 1902 until the horrific persecution of 1922, he was nurtured with the spiritual springs and traditions of the piety of Asia Minor.

As a child, he would go to the chapels on the islands in front of the harbor, and when he returned, he would ask his mother, "Mother, who is the woman holding the child in her arms inside the church?"

"Our Lady the Panagia," she would reply sweetly, "with the Lord Christ."

From a young age, the elder saw tangibly in his life the protection of the Panagia and her guidance. At the age of fifteen, he volunteered for the allied army, burning with zeal for the vision of Greater Greece. Then, in a shipwreck in the Mediterranean, he was miraculously saved by the Panagia and Saint Nicholas, after battling the elements for three days and nights in the open sea.

In Mytilene, where he settled after the Asia Minor catastrophe, his consolation was the Panagia of Agiasos. The vows he had made to her as a fisherman and sailor, he later repaid as a monk, thus expressing his thanks and gratitude for her help. He recounted:

> In 1928, I was traveling with our caïque [fishing boat] off Tinos. The weather was good, and the caïque was running at eight miles.
>
> "Hey Anthony," I said to my brother, "I wish to venerate the Panagia." He, however, refused: "We won't find such weather again. We will be in Piraeus in the morning."
>
> What could I say? Anthony was my elder. So I walked around on the deck until we approached three hundred to four hundred meters from the harbor. Then suddenly the wind died. The sea became like oil around the caïque. The sails hung limp. But what a strange thing! The calm was only for us. Farther out, the wind was roaring. It was, it seems, an intervention of the Panagia, to satisfy my desire.
>
> "Alright, have it your way," said Anthony.
>
> It was Pascha. We went ashore and venerated. There I heard for the first time "The Angel Cried."

Later, the Panagia in a wondrous manner called Father Gelasius from his caïque to her garden (the Holy Mountain). The elder recounted:

> One night in my sleep, it seemed to me that many people were gathered to welcome the queen. From afar, the horses appeared, running, pulling behind them a golden chariot. Upon it sat the queen with a multitude of attendants and officers. Suddenly, someone grabbed me and lifted me onto the chariot, at the back. Soon we arrived at a castle with towers and a splendid palace. There the queen alighted. However, I didn't get a clear look at her. I

only noticed one side of her face as she ascended the palace stairs.

I woke up! I went out and went to the coffee shop, where other sailors were. I was in Pasalimani with my loaded caïque. But my mind was filled with the beauty of the queen.

Later, I met a monk from Saint Anne's. I recounted my dream to him, and he explained to me that the Panagia was calling me to the Holy Mountain to become her faithful follower.

My heart was divided for a little while. But the love of the queen prevailed. That same day, I too, like the Apostles, abandoned a loaded ship, brother, parents, and set out for Athos. The end of my journey was the Monastery of Grigoriou. I entered the katholikon to venerate. At that moment, the Divine Liturgy was being chanted. In the Theotokos icon of the iconostasis, I recognized the queen of my dream! I hastened to kiss it, whereupon Deacon Theodore, who was standing there, told me, "Are the icons of the Panagia lost, my child, that you came to the iconostasis to venerate?" But, of course, how could he know what was in my own heart?

[16]

The Blasphemous Fisherman

In Piso Livadi, on the island of Paros, on the day before the eve of the Dormition of the Theotokos in 1931, there were three groups of fishermen who fished at night with their grigri (purse seine boats) in the strait between Paros and Naxos.

That night, one group stayed in the small harbor. The fishermen indulged in drink, the drink brought high spirits, and that led to misunderstandings and harsh words. The blasphemers did not even respect the Panagia. In vain did the harbor master and the shopkeeper of the small port try to restrain them.

Suddenly the sky grew heavy. The sea began to roar. In half an hour, the wave rose like a mountain, sweeping away the fishing boat and the smaller boats with their lamps, until it threw them broken onto the shore. Afterwards, the sea calmed, and a caïque from Naxos was seen entering the small harbor. Its captain was astonished to see the wreckage on the shore.

"How did this happen?" he asked. "I was sailing on a sea like glass!"

"It was a miracle of the Panagia," explained one of the gri-gri fishermen.

Most agreed. Two or three, however, spoke ironically and gave another explanation: "It was a whirlwind. It's a good thing it didn't lift our boats into the sky."

One, in particular, Gregory Liakouras, added, "Come on, as if it was a miracle! The Panagia—may I not 'adorn' her now with curses—wasn't in the mood to bother with us fishermen."

This he said and went to see the damage his own fishing boat had suffered. He found it smashed to pieces. He then spat furiously on the wreckage, blasphemed the Panagia again, and retired to sleep.

As soon as he lay down, he saw the Panagia vividly—as if in a dream, yet as if awake—approaching him and asking him, "Why, my child, do you not respect me?"

"What are these things you're telling me, lady?" he fumed. "I don't know you at all. When did I not respect you?"

"You don't know me? Then why do you always blaspheme me?"

At these words, he sprang upright. He tried to shout, to run, but he couldn't. His feet had sunk up to his knees in the

Panagia Ekatontapyliani,
Monastery of Panagia Ekatontapyliani, Parikia, Paros (Greece)

sand. He made the sign of the cross. And then he saw again, clearly now, the Panagia and heard her say to him, "Come to my house, to Ekatontapyliani [the Church with the Hundred Doors], in Parikia of Paros. Come there to venerate me."

Liakouras left at that very moment, almost running. He arrived at Ekatontapyliani shortly after sunrise. He ran quickly to the icon of the Theotokos. In her divine form, he recognized the woman of his vision. He knelt and prayed for entire hours. Then he returned to Piso Livadi. There he discovered a new miracle: the boats and the fishing vessel stood on the shore without any damage!

[21]

An Abortion That Did Not Happen

The first children Eutychia Alexandrou bore were boys, but they did not survive. Afterwards, she only brought girls into the world. In 1939, she moved with her family to Khartoum, Sudan. There she became pregnant again, but distressed by her previous experiences, she decided to have an abortion.

That same night, she saw a shocking dream. It was Good Friday, and she was preparing to enter the Orthodox church of the Evangelistria in Khartoum. At that moment, the priest, dressed in his vestments and holding the Holy Gospel, said to her, "You are sinful!"

Immediately, Eutychia knelt, greatly moved, and asked for forgiveness. Then the priest led her inside the church, to where the Epitaphios (funerary bier of Christ) was, and said to her, "I am not worthy to forgive you. From this One you must ask for forgiveness."

The woman turned and saw near the Epitaphios the icon of the Panagia weeping. Real tears flowed from her divine eyes. At some point, she turned towards Eutychia and said to her, "Look! I had One, and I lost Him. Be careful not to lose the one you carry within you."

Afterwards, the priest took a large cross from around his neck, placed it on hers, and told her, "Be careful not to lose the cross you wear."

When she awoke, she recalled the dream in every detail. By this, she was convinced that she had to keep her child at all costs.

In five months, she gave birth to a baby boy. With astonishment, she saw imprinted on his sternum the sign of the Holy Cross. She then vowed to the Panagia to bring the little one and baptize him in Tinos. Unfortunately, the

Second World War intervened, and she was forced to baptize him in Khartoum. However, she did not fail to name him Evangelos.

As the child grew up, he learned from his mother the story of his birth, and the desire to venerate the Most Gracious Lady took root within him.

One year, at the feast of the Panagia, young Evangelos also came to Tinos as a pilgrim with his mother. He even wanted to stay all night in the church, because he desired and believed he would see the Panagia. The Great Vespers had progressed, and the bishop was preaching under the central chandelier. Suddenly, Evangelos saw from the women's gallery, where he was, a strong light that shone like the sun and sometimes took on a red hue. At the same time, he saw a beautiful young woman approaching. She had a regal bearing, wore a halo, and with her right hand raised, she blessed the crowds.

[35]

The Witch's Chickpeas

In our time, magic has been adorned with many euphemistic adjectives to more easily deceive the naive. However, we must clarify that under whatever guise magic is practiced, it is one of the methods the devil uses to deceive man, to distance him from God, and to crush him physically and mentally. Let us see this truth in the following incident:

A certain woman, married in Athens, did not live harmoniously with her husband because he was unfaithful to her. People then recommended a witch to her, who would supposedly solve her problem. The witch read some magic spells for her and gave her nine chickpeas to keep in her house.

From then on, however, she constantly had nightmares while sleeping. She continually saw a savage man with a hideous appearance, who threatened to kill her.

Time passed. One day, while walking in front of the holy church of Kapnikarea in Athens, she saw that they were selling icons of Panagia Eikosifoinissa (copies of the miraculous icon kept in the monastery of the same name near Drama). She bought one icon and prayed to the Panagia, begging her never to see that nightly nightmare again.

That evening, however, the savage man reappeared in her sleep. She then cried out, "My Panagia, help me and save me!" At the same moment, she saw a woman with a child in her arms appearing at her door. Terrified, she shouted at her, "Go away! You are a bad person too!"

The savage man, meanwhile, as soon as he saw the woman with the baby—who was none other than the Panagia—immediately disappeared. Then the Theotokos entered her room and told her, "I am not a bad person. I am the Panagia. This man comes here and frightens you because you possess the chickpeas. Throw them away, and he will not come again. When you wake up, look at the iconostasis, and you will see my icon."

Indeed, when she woke up, she saw the icon of the Panagia on the iconostasis, where she had placed it the previous day. She immediately threw away the chickpeas, and the nightmare stopped.

Of course, the chickpeas were not to blame for her problem, but the fact that she kept them in her room, obeying and showing absolute trust in the witch, the instrument of Satan. Thus she was denying Christ, the one Who "undoes the works of the devil." This, however, gave rights to Satan and freed his hands to terrorize her.

[8]

Divine Consolations

The ascetic life of Elder Joseph the Hesychast (+1959)—the monk who struggled on the front line of the zealots of the Holy Mountain—was distinguished from its beginning. It was characterized by harsh spiritual struggle, which resulted in fierce temptations from demons, but also intense consolations from divine grace. This is evident in the following incidents, which he himself narrated:

> The time I was practicing asceticism in Vigla, I experienced a strong temptation. I then resorted with tears to prayer, with some complaint towards God for the lack of His help. I also addressed the Most Holy Theotokos and pleaded with her. Suddenly, as I was turned towards Athos, I saw coming out of the chapel of the Panagia a bright ray, forming something like a rainbow and resting upon me. Immediately I felt a physical and spiritual transformation, and I began to say the prayer rhythmically and completely effortlessly. I was flooded with light, spiritual fragrance, and joy. And after I was sufficiently comforted, the pure white light withdrew to its original place.
>
> Another time, while I was experiencing the violence of a fierce temptation, I suddenly felt my heart flooded with divine love. It was as if I then found myself in a plain and was walking lightly. Walking, I heard conversations. I turned and saw a general speaking to me with great familiarity and saying, "Welcome, Father Joseph. I was expecting you. Come in to venerate."
>
> Immediately he took me by the hand, we descended a luxurious staircase, and found ourselves

Saint Joseph the Hesychast

in a magnificent church. The church had most beautiful stalls full of luminous young men, who were chanting melodious hymns. These young men invited me to approach and treated me with great intimacy. "Come, Father Joseph, let us go to venerate," said my guide. And after leading me before the icon of the Panagia, he took a pleading tone and said, "Lady, show your glory to your servant, lest he be overwhelmed by sorrow."

I then saw the Panagia no longer as an icon, but alive and in her full form, holding the Savior in her embrace. I could not bear her divine glory and fell to the ground.

"Lady, Lady," I whispered, weeping, "do not abandon me."

With her honey-sweet and comforting voice, she then said to my guide, "Take him now to his place to struggle and have his hope in me." Since then, this phrase has been my constant consolation.

For a time, I was living in quietude in the desert of Little Saint Anne's skete. Once when temptations and sorrows multiplied, I entered the chapel of the kalyvi (cell or house), proceeded to the icon of the Panagia, and begged her, weeping. I then saw the icon flash and the Theotokos take on normal dimensions. I saw her before me alive, in her full form, super-luminous, and sun-like. I bowed before her, unable to gaze at her any longer, and heard her say to me, "Did I not tell you to have your hope in me? Why are you discouraged?"

Then she leaned slightly towards me, whereupon the Divine Infant extended His little hand and caressed my head and forehead three times. Immediately my soul was flooded with love, consolation, and light. I could no longer stand on my feet. I fell to the ground and with longing kissed the spot where the Queen of All had stood, for she had already returned to her icon. This spot exuded fragrance for a long time, constantly reminding me of her blessed promise.

[18]

A Garden of the Panagia

In the Bistritsa valley of Romania, the Monastery was founded during the sixteenth century. There exists a small icon of the Theotokos, known and revered by the surrounding inhabitants. In this valley, hermits had lived from ancient times. Some of them were scandalized because other, younger monks were building cells and churches with stone and not with wood, as they had been accustomed to until then. They thought that this practice would alter their monastic spirit and they would lose their souls. So, they set out for Athos.

Panagia of Biserichani,
Biserichani Monastery, Romania

The Panagia of Biserichani, however, performed her miracle. As they were walking, she appeared before them dressed in white and told them, "Turn back. This place here is also my garden."

The monks obeyed and returned. Later, at the spot of the appearance, they built a shrine.

[13]

The Unexpected Blessing

During the years of the German occupation, hunger plagued the entire country. The monks of the Holy Mountain were also tested, but they could clearly see the help of the Most Holy Theotokos.

It was August 1942, and the Paraklesis services to the Panagia had begun. In New Skete, the miller Father Arsenius Mantzarolas had no flour at all. Furthermore, he owed twenty borrowed loaves of bread to fathers of the skete. And because he could not return them, he was ashamed even to see them. He was so saddened that he decided to leave the Holy Mountain at dawn on August 13 and slowly make his way on foot to his homeland, Sparta.

The evening before, fasting and distressed, he lay down a little to rest. As soon as he fell asleep, it seemed to him that he saw his mother.

"What is wrong, my child, that you are so sad?"

"Mother, I have no bread at all. What else would you have me possess? Mother, I am hungry!"

"And for this, you want to leave the Mountain?"

"Yes, for this."

"And where do you plan to go, unfortunate child? Am I not—for centuries now—the Governess of the Mountain? How is it possible for me to break my promise? See, I have brought you a caïque with wheat to the shore. Go and take some."

"Mother, how can I buy wheat since I have no money?"

"Go down to old Symeon, and he will give you some. He too is distressed because he has no wheat. But he has his hope in me. Tell him, then, and all the fathers to go down and buy."

When the monks went down to the shore, they found the sailors sitting outside at Kalamia.

"Fathers," they said, "we don't have wheat for sale. The Germans forced us to transport war material from Kavala to Kolyndros, and they gave each of us three hundred okades (approximately 384 kg) of wheat as payment. However, because we see that you too are in great need, we will donate to each of you thirty okades (approximately 38.4 kg)."

The monks thanked the sailors and glorified God for the unexpected boon. After calculating how many okades they needed, they left with the boat for the caïque, weighed the wheat, brought it to the shore, and distributed it to the monks.

"Fathers," the sailors then said, "the Germans want us to leave at midnight. They are afraid for us to set out during the day. Until then, could we come to venerate the holy relics?"

The monks gladly accepted and all set out for the kyriakon (main church of the skete). Arriving at the shrine, the captain asked, "We need a little coffee. Can you give us one or two okades, and we will pay you with wheat?"

"Agreed," they replied. "We bought the coffee for fifty drachmas an okada, while the wheat is ten. So you will give us five okades of wheat for each okada of coffee."

"No," said the captain. "You will take twenty okades of wheat for each okada of coffee."

"But this is not fair," disagreed Father Iakovos. "The Lord Christ does not desire this."

"Fathers," the captain then said, "whatever wheat we have in our caïque will remain here, so that all the monks of the skete may be provided for."

Then they all proceeded to the kyriakon, where a fervent thanksgiving and an all-night vigil followed in honor of the Most Holy Theotokos and for the peace of the whole world. And the sailors, after venerating the holy relics left for their caique and deeply moved.

[2]

The Blasphemous Actor

In Heliopolis of Phoenicia, around the sixth century A.D., lived an actor named Gaianus. This man, when he appeared in the theater, would mock and blaspheme the Most Holy Theotokos. So, the Theotokos appears to him in his sleep and said to him, "What harm have I done to you, that you slander me and blaspheme me before so many people?"

But even after this admonition, the actor was not corrected. On the contrary, he blasphemed even more. The Panagia appeared to him three more times and admonished him with the same words. He, however, remained uncorrected and blasphemed her all the more.

Then, one afternoon, while he was sleeping, the Panagia appeared to him again and, without saying anything, traced a line with her finger on his hands and feet. When the actor awoke, he found himself with his hands and feet severed. The pedagogical punishment here on earth would help him to avoid eternal hell.

[17]

The Panagia and the Baker

In the holy Monastery of Saint Paul, at the beginning of the twentieth century, lived a good-natured little elder, Elder Thomas. He served in the monastery's bakery as an assistant to Elder Gregory, who was the responsible kneader and baker.

Once, Elder Gregory was absent for two days and left his ever-willing and obedient assistant as his replacement in the service. Elder Thomas, however, had never kneaded alone and was taken aback. He had to prepare and provide bread for sixty monks and for ten to twenty pilgrims.

In this hour of need, he began to pray fervently to the Panagia and to Saint Paul to enlighten him on what to do, because he did not know where to begin. He took the leaven, and while he was preparing to add water and flour, he saw beside him a majestic woman dressed in black.

The monk was at a loss. She went forward, took the leaven, and mixed it in the kneading trough with water and flour. In two hours, she had the dough ready, shaped the loaves, baked them, and in another two hours, took them out of the oven.

Elder Thomas watched as if hypnotized. He could not understand how all this had happened. The only thing he understood was that the black-clad woman was none other than the Panagia. When the monks ate of this bread, they asked him, "Elder Thomas, how did you manage to knead so quickly? What did you put in the dough that made the bread so sweet and tasty?"

Some of them to this day still remember its deliciousness and sweetness. In this way, the Lady Theotokos revealed to the monks that she cares for them as a mother cares for her children.

[2]

The Holy Martyrs of Zographou

Since the Holy Mountain had always been the bastion and support of Orthodoxy in the East, the Latins wished to destroy it and establish the Pope's authority there as well.

So, in 1280, they entered the Holy Mountain with military force and devoted themselves to their work, sometimes with promises and money, and other times with threats, violence, and tortures.

Some cowards succumbed. Most monks, however, refused the Pope's authority as Christ's vicar, as well as his unsound dogmas; for this reason, they sealed their confession with their blood. In this endeavor of theirs, the Latins unfortunately had as their collaborators Emperor Michael Palaiologos and Patriarch John Beccus.

After doing what they did in the other monasteries, they finally passed by the Monastery of Zographou. During that period, a monk, who had the habit of reading the Salutations to the Theotokos many times a day before her icon, was practicing asceticism near the monastery.

One day, while the archangelic salutation was sounding on the elder's lips, he suddenly heard from the holy icon the phrase, "Rejoice, you too, Elder of God!" The elder was terrified. "Do not be afraid!" continued the quiet voice of the Theotokos, which came from the icon. "Go quickly, however, to the monastery, and tell the abbot and the monks that my enemies and the enemies of my Son have approached. Whoever, therefore, is weak in spirit, let him go and hide until the temptation passes. But whoever desires martyrs' crowns, let them remain in the monastery. Go quickly!"

The elder set off immediately, obedient to the command of the Theotokos. And as soon as he reached the monastery, he saw with astonishment at the gate the icon of the Panagia, before which he had been reading the Salutations a little while ago. He knelt with compunction, kissed the icon, and presented himself with it to the abbot.

The monks were disturbed by the terrible news. Some ran and hid in the mountains and caves. Twenty-six,

Fresco depicting the twenty-six martyrs, located in the large katholikon of Zographou Monastery, Mt. Athos (Greece)

however—and with them the abbot—remained in the monastery, ascended the tower, and awaited there the enemies and the martyrs' crowns.

Soon the Latins also arrived. At first, they employed all of their rhetorical skill to persuade the monks to open the gates and recognize the Pope as head of the universal Church.

"And who told you that the Pope is the head of the Church?" shouted the monks. "The head of the Church is Christ! We are not opening the gates. We prefer to die rather than let you defile this holy place!"

"Since you wish it, you shall die!" shouted the Latins with fury. And immediately they gathered wood and brushwood around the tower, lit a fire, and burned them all.

[41]

PART IV

PROTECTRESS AND HELPER

Little Lake Prespa, on the Greek-Albanian border,
with the ruined basilica of Saint Achillius in the foreground.

In the War of 1940

On the front, all along the line, from the blue sea of the Ionian to the high, frozen Prespes, the Greek army began to see the same vision everywhere. They saw at night a female figure advancing—tall, slender, and light-footed—with her veil thrown back from her head to her shoulders. They recognized her, they knew her from old; her praises had been sung to them when they were infants dreaming in their cradles. She was the magnanimous mother in pain and in glory, the wounded one of Tinos, the Champion Leader.

[34]

Letter from Morova

Tasos Rigopoulos, who was serving in Albania in 1940, sent the following letter from the front to his brother.

> My brother Nikos,
>
> I am writing to you from an eagle's nest, four hundred meters higher than the peak of Parnitha. Nature all around is pure white. My purpose, however, is not to describe to you the charms of a snow-covered Morova with all its wild majesty. My purpose is to convey to you what I experienced, what I saw with my own eyes, and what I fear lest, hearing it from others, you will not believe.

A few moments before we charged the fortifications of Morova, we saw, at a distance of about ten meters, a tall, black-clad woman standing motionless.

"Who are you?"

Silence. The guard, angry, shouted again, "Who are you?"

Then, as if an electric current passed through us all, we whispered, "**The Panagia!**"

She rushed forward as if she had eagle's wings. We followed behind her. We constantly felt her instilling bravery in us. For a whole week, we fought hard to capture the Ivan-Morova fortifications.

I emphasize that our attack caught the Italians during the changeover of their units. The old detachments had withdrawn, and the new ones... were sleeping! What happened to them cannot be described. She always charged ahead. And when, victorious, we were rolling down towards the undefended Korçë, then the Champion Leader became vapor, a soft cloud, and disappeared.

[29]

Miracle at Boubesi

A vivid miracle of the Panagia was experienced during the Greco-Italian war by the soldiers of the Fifty-first Independent Battalion, commanded by Major Petrakis, on the crest of Rondeni, to the right of the legendary Kleisoura.

Every night, from January 22, 1941, onwards, at exactly 9:20 p.m., the heavy Italian artillery would begin firing upon Petrakis's battalion and the road through which the transport vehicles passed. Days passed, and the trouble continued, causing nervousness and casualties. Daring scouts from the vanguard and airmen were dispatched deep into the Italian lines but returned unsuccessful. They could not locate the Italian artillery, perhaps because the Italians relocated them every night.

However, it was absolutely necessary to locate the enemy positions. One evening in February, the volleys of the Italian cannons were heard again. "My Panagia," the major shouted quite spontaneously, "help us! Save us from these demons."

Immediately, a luminous cloud appeared in the distance. Slowly, it formed something like a halo. And beneath it, some silvery clouds formed the figure of the Panagia, who began to lean towards the earth and came to rest in a ravine between two heights of Boubesi. Everyone in the battalion saw the vision and shivered.

"Miracle!" shouted the major.

"Miracle! Miracle!" repeated the soldiers and crossed themselves.

Immediately, a liaison officer left with a note from Petrakis for Tzimas's artillery battery. In ten minutes, the Greek cannons thundered, and within twenty, the Italian ones fell silent. Our shells had perfectly hit the target.

[21]

The Blasphemous Warrant Officer

Christos Vergos, conscripted in the Korean War, recounts:

> I was a warrant officer in the Korean battalion. I believed in nothing except the power of the heavy weapons I commanded. Furthermore, I was incorrigibly blasphemous. All my blasphemies were directed at the Panagia. Those who heard me shuddered. My soldiers made the sign of the

cross, lest evil befall them. My superiors constantly reprimanded and punished me. Until one night I experienced an undeniable miracle.

Dawn was breaking on April 7, 1951. With my platoon, I had occupied a slope on a hill near the 38th parallel. Until dawn, I remained awake in my trench with Private Stavros Adamakos. When dawn was breaking, at which point there was no fear of surprise attack, I fell asleep. I then had a dream that shook me up:

A woman dressed in black, with pure beauty and a very sweet voice, approached me and, touching my shoulder, asked, "Do you want me to be near you, Christos?"

I then felt a deep exultation.

"And who are you?" I asked her.

Then she changed expression and reprimanded me sternly: "Why, Christos, do you constantly curse me?"

"It's the first time I've seen you!" I protested. "How is it possible for me to curse someone I don't know?"

"Yes, Christos," she insisted more sternly. "You curse me. But I am always near you and all the soldiers of the battalion. Why don't you go to Pusan, to light candles for your brothers who are buried there?"

With this phrase, I woke up terrified. Stavros beside me looked at me bewildered.

"Sir, something is wrong with you," he told me. "You were groaning and talking in your sleep."

I recounted my dream to him, and we concluded it was the result of fatigue and discussions about the dead of Pusan.

However, while we were saying this, I saw again the woman from my dream before me.

"Adamakos!" I shouted. "The woman. This one... Do you see her?"

He tried to calm me, but to no avail! The black-clad woman with the pure beauty and the very sweet voice stood near me and told me, "Don't be afraid... Don't be afraid, my child. I am the Panagia. I protect you all everywhere and always. But I want from you not to curse me even in the most difficult moments of your life."

Agitated, I immediately fell down to kiss her feet. But she had vanished. I then wept from the depths of my heart a cry of relief and joy, I who had never cried in my life.

[21]

The Stray Mule

From the war of 1940, N. Dramountianos recounts his wondrous experience:

Our company received an order to occupy an advanced height for a bridgehead. We set up defenses among the rocks. As soon as we were settled, heavy snow began to fall. It fell continuously for two days and nights and in many places reached two meters. We were cut off from supplies. Each of us had food in his backpack for one day. From hunger and cold, we took no thought for the morrow and devoured it.

From then on, the torment began. We quenched our thirst with snow, but hunger gnawed at us. We spent five days and nights like this. We became skeletons. We kept our morale high, but nature has its limits. Some succumbed. We all expected the same end, "for faith and fatherland."

Then an inspiration from our captain brought about the miracle! He took from his bosom a paper icon of the Panagia, set it up on the high ground, and called us around him:

"My brave lads!" he said. "In this critical situation, only a miracle can save us. Kneel, pray to the Panagia, the mother of the God-man, to help us!"

We fell to our knees, raised our hands, prayed fervently. We hadn't even stood up when we heard bells. We were surprised and grabbed our weapons. We took aim.

Not a minute passed before we saw a huge mule approaching, fully laden. We leaped for joy! An animal without a guide, crossing the mountain with at least a meter of snow, was completely unnatural. We understood: the Lady Theotokos was guiding it. We all thanked her together, softly but wholeheartedly chanting "To the Champion Leader" and other hymns to her. The animal had a whole supply of food on it: rusks, cheeses, canned goods, cognac, and more.

Many and unbelievable hardships I endured in the war. But this one remains unforgettable for me because there was no way out. Yet the Panagia provided it.

[10]

The Rescue of the Convoy

Kostantis Haropoulos, an old seadog, now spends his days in his privately-owned hotel, reminiscing about the old times. He once recounted the following miracle:

During the period of the American-Japanese war, I was working as a first engineer on an oil tanker of the merchant fleet. We loaded unrefined petroleum for airplanes from an Indian base and set off for a large island in the Pacific, which was an American airbase. However, we traveled with our souls in our teeth, because Japanese submarines were hunting us, causing terrible damage. We had destroyers around us, of course, but the Japanese would sneak in from underneath, pass the defensive screen, and hit us with torpedoes. It was mayhem.

This time, we also had an unusual storm. The waves rose like mountains. The destroyers bobbed like walnuts here and there. We thought our end had come.

"Make the sign of the cross!" I shouted to the captain and the crew. "Pray for the Almighty to help."

"God Almighty, save us! In this chaos, only You can help."

"Amen!" everyone shouted.

The sea slowly began to calm. But we hadn't even caught our breath when a cyclone hit us.

"Hard to port and full speed ahead!" roared the captain. "All hands to your stations!"

The engines were about to break from the shaking and the overheating. Fortunately, the cyclone only grazed us peripherally. We glorified the Almighty again. Drenched in sweat, I went up from the engine room to have a coffee. I hadn't even taken a sip when I suddenly saw the third engineer dart in front of me to announce that the engines were spewing fire. I quickly leaped into the hold, grabbed the fire hose, and directed water at the source of the fire. But what a tragic irony! I don't know how, but the hose wrapped around me and squeezed me like a boa constrictor on a deer. I struggled to untangle myself, but it was impossible. A little longer, and I would have suffocated. In my agony, I thought of the fire that would spread to the entire convoy, and I shouted, "My Panagia Ekatontapyliani, save us in this final hour!"

That was it. The hose, in an inexplicable way, loosened. I took a deep breath and continued extinguishing the fire. When I finished, the entire crew came. They embraced me tearfully and kissed me. I then stood serious and with great emotion told them, "Dear colleagues, what happened was a miracle of Panagia Ekatontapyliani. In the utmost danger, I called upon her, and she saved both me and the entire convoy from certain death." I explained to them how it happened, and everyone made the sign of the cross.

[10]

The Tractor

The venerable abbot of the Holy Monastery of Stavrovouni, Cyprus, Archimandrite Athanasius, as he himself states in a relevant article, has been benefited many times in his life by the Most Holy Theotokos. The following incident, an undeniable miracle, constitutes for him a small sample of her intervention:

It was February 9, 1960, and my late Elder Germanos gave me an order to drive the monastery's tractor from our metochion (dependency) of Saint Modestos to the metochion of Saint Barbara. It was the leavetaking of the feast of the Presentation of the

Lord, and as I was driving, I was chanting in honor of the Panagia: "Incomprehensible is that which is wrought in you, both to angels and to mortals, O Mother-Virgin Pure," and "Theotokos, the hope of all Christians, protect, guard, keep those who hope in you."

Suddenly, while I was in front of a downhill slope, the tractor went out of my control, and its speed increased dangerously. Some malfunction had occurred, and I was not a skilled enough driver to make the necessary maneuvers. The brakes were not working, nor could I manage to change gears. At any moment, there was a risk of overturning, resulting in some serious injury or even death itself.

Immediately, I entrusted all my hope to the Most Holy Theotokos.

"My Panagia, help me! My Panagia, save me!" I shouted in agony.

The tractor was rapidly approaching the riverbank. According to human calculations, I had only a few moments of life left. But O, your wonders, Most Blessed Theotokos! The tractor, after plunging into some bushes, stopped unexpectedly right at the edge of the river and of destruction.

I thanked the Ever-Virgin from the depths of my soul for hearing the cry of my supplication. Afterwards, I got off the machine and went on foot to the metochion of Saint Barbara, where I met my Elder.

"I almost got killed!" I told him. "The tractor stopped at the last moment by the grace of the Panagia. My obedience to my Elder and the protection of the Theotokos, to whom I was chanting the megalynaria, saved me."

Near the riverbank was a large pine tree. In a crevice of it, I placed an icon of the Panagia. And every time we passed by there, we would stop for a little while to venerate.

[1]

The Panagia's Deer

The Monastery of Panagia of Mesovouni was hidden, during the years of Turkish rule, behind a high mountain, to the left of the road that goes from the Thessalian plain to Arta. Its path was dangerous; only goats and local villagers could cross it. Everyone spoke of the old glory of the monastery and its splendor. In the dark years of slavery, however, it too was steeped in poverty.

The monastery celebrated its feast day every year on September 8, the Nativity of the Theotokos. It was the most splendid festival in the region of Argithea. And the monks had the custom of slaughtering a calf, boiling it in the cauldrons of the kitchen, and after the church service, distributing it as a blessing to the faithful.

The annual festival had for years ceased to be celebrated with splendor. The monastery did not even have an animal to offer. This saddened many. They considered it bad luck, as well as contempt for the Panagia. "What can we do?" the abbot would respond to them. "Not even a rooster is left."

Among those who were saddened was an old monk, white-bearded, approaching eighty years of age. "Perform your miracle, my Panagia!" he pleaded day and night to the Theotokos. "Perform any miracle, to show your people that you are near them, so they do not lose their faith in you."

Dawn was breaking on the feast of the Dormition. The old monk was resting in his cell when suddenly a vision shook him. Before the semantron for Matins sounded, he

Monastery of Panagia of Mesovouni,
dedicated to the Nativity of the Virgin Mary (church rebuilt in 1904),
Mesovouni, Greece

got up and went to the abbot. He knocked loudly on the door.

"What brings you here at such an hour, blessed one?"

"My Elder, I saw a living and divine vision. A little while ago, my cell was illuminated by an abundant light. Before I could fully recover, I saw the Panagia standing before me. She looked at me sternly, but also with love. She seemed pained, but also full of serenity. I then heard her say to me, 'Tell the abbot and the brothers to celebrate my memory festively this year. For the worst of what this people has lost is their faith. Let the villages gather for my sake, and I will be with them.' Immediately afterwards, she disappeared."

The abbot heard the vision with attention, but also with hesitation. Then he set off for the church.

From the nearby village, several pilgrims had come. By word of mouth, the monk's vision became known, and soon it was also known in the other villages of the region. The holiness of his life was a reliable testimony. Even the bishop held him as an example.

Some approached the abbot and begged him to carry out the will of the Theotokos, since she had made it known in such a vivid way. So, a week after the leave-taking of the Dormition, on the feast of the Beheading of the Honorable Forerunner, monks and villagers heard from the abbot's mouth the joyful news: "By the grace and blessing of the Panagia, our monastery will have a splendid festival this year, such as has not been held for many years. However, you know that times are difficult and the monastery is poor. Therefore, this time we will not have a slaughtered animal. But we will gather to celebrate."

The news immediately fluttered over mountains and plains; it became known in all the surrounding villages. At last, they would again have the splendid festival of the Panagia. They would gather again under her grace. It could only be for good. Perhaps God was preparing better days for the nation and for everyone.

From the very eve of the feast, the whole plateau to the right of the monastery began to fill with people. Groups upon groups of pilgrims arrived from the surrounding villages, through the steep slopes and forests. All the priests of the villages also came, and a magnificent liturgy took place. The people had spread out on the slopes because they could not fit in the small church. The service would be very long. At the end, nine priests, splendidly robed, would come out with the icon of the Panagia for the Artoklasia (the service of the blessing of the five loaves).

Suddenly, while everyone was sitting and waiting, they heard a commotion from the slope of the wooded hill. They then turned and saw a deer approaching boldly and with a swift pace. It was so unexpected that no one thought to do anything. As if guided by an invisible hand, it passed through the crowd and bounded through the main gate. Then, as if it were an animal of the monastery that knew its way around, it proceeded directly to the kitchen. There it stopped.

The monk who was there serving the pilgrims did not know what to do. First of all, he gave it water. The deer drank with all its soul. After quenching its thirst, it lay down in a corner and stretched out its neck in such a way, as if offering itself for a sacrifice.

"A gift from the Panagia!" said the older people. She had, after all, announced it through the old monk. The abbot was immediately notified. He too agreed that they should slaughter the deer and distribute it to the people as a blessing from the Panagia.

And so it happened. That year, all the pilgrims received their share at noon. They experienced an undeniable miracle. Hundreds of eyes saw it. Hundreds of mouths confessed it. The news, like lightning, electrified the villages of Argithea.

Since then, every year on the feast day of the Panagia, September 8, a deer always came before the monastery gate. No one saw it wandering in the mountains beforehand. But it always came on its day, at its hour, to its place, in her grace. It would cool off, rest, and then lie down on the ground and offer its neck to the knife.

Years later, the Turks left the country. The monks who first witnessed the miracle also died. Others took their place. The miracle, however, continued.

One year, at the festival, the deer was nowhere to be seen. Matins finished, they entered the liturgy, and the people began to worry.

"Our sins are to blame!" said the pilgrims.

"People have begun to stray again, to lose their faith," others added.

But just as the Cherubic Hymn began, there was the deer again. The crowd was relieved. The monk, who was waiting with the knife in his hand, breathed a sigh of relief. The deer, as if lost, looked right and left fearfully, and then headed for the monastery. It arrived at the gate sweating and panting. The monk and the cooks immediately grabbed it and slaughtered it. They would barely have time to prepare it for noon.

"The deer will not come again," said a hundred-year-old shepherd. "We showed ourselves hard-hearted. We only looked after our own convenience. We didn't let it rest and quench its thirst, but led it immediately to slaughter. We sinned."

No one paid attention to the elder's words. But when the next year the deer did not appear at all, then they understood they were at fault. Since then, the deer never appeared again.

Years passed. Other antichrists came, who destroyed the monastery and exterminated the monks. Today, nothing remains of the old magnificent monastery except for the small church and the ruined kitchen. And yet, every year, on September 8, the villages of Argithea gather there and celebrate her grace. And they wait for the deer to reappear as in the old days—a miracle of the Panagia of Mesovouni to the enslaved nation.

[22]

The Snakes of Cephalonia

In southern Cephalonia, near the village of Markopoulo, stands the church of the Dormition. There, during every Dormition fast, something strange and wondrous takes place. From the feast of the Transfiguration onwards, snakes appear inside and outside the church. These are called "the Panagia's snakes."

As the days pass, they multiply, and on the eve of the Dormition, they increase excessively. You see the inhabitants of Markopoulo wandering in the ravine—on the bank of which the church is built—to gather snakes to bring to the Panagia. Where they come from, and also where they hide after the feast, no one knows. It remains a mystery.

During Vespers, they move freely among the faithful, on the icon stands and in the church stalls, without fearing anyone. "They will climb into your bosom," the villagers say to prepare strangers, "and by the grace of the Panagia, they will not harm you. You will hold them in your hand, and they will lick you like kittens."

This event is emphasized by the following local couplet:

The snakes from Markopoulo, I wish they would eat me,
but they belong to the Panagia and they caress me.

Snakes of Cephalonia

Indeed, one sees unbelievable things. Some snakes wrap like bracelets on the arms of the faithful. Others climb on the icon of the Panagia or on the Crucifix, and others on the loaves of the Artoklasia (breaking of bread service). A snake might also climb onto the Gospel book that the priest is reading during the Divine Liturgy. They too celebrate, as representatives of the animal kingdom, along with the Christians. And they give the feast an Edenic tone, since in Eden the first-formed humans lived in brotherhood with the animals.

With the passing of August 15, the snakes also depart. German naturalists examined them but could not classify them into any of the known species. They are gray, thin, and do not exceed a meter in length. When you stroke them, you feel their skin is velvety, and you see two sparkling little eyes. On their broad head, a small cross is formed, as it is also on the tip of their thin tongue.

If one year the snakes do not appear, it is a bad sign. This happened in 1940, as well as in 1953, when the island was tested by earthquakes.

[12]

A Miracle Under the Microscope

An unprecedented miracle of the Theotokos stirred the religious world in France. Bassam Assaf was a servant of an Orthodox Syrian in Paris, Michael Merez.

On August 12, 1988, Merez was absent and telephoned Assaf to make the necessary preparations for the feast of the Dormition. The wealthy businessman had a small chapel within his house. In it, the faithful servant burned incense, lit an unceasing oil lamp, and offered flowers to the Theotokos, of whom there are many icons there.

Afterwards, he prayed to the Panagia for his family living in Syria, and for his master whom he loved like a father. At that very moment, the Theotokos appeared to the servant and said to him, "I protect you. I am with you. Take this gift!" At the same moment, Assaf felt his hands fill with a liquid that had the consistency and aroma of very pure olive oil.

When Merez returned to Paris, he was informed of the event but preferred to keep it secret. However, the miracle was repeated, and the miraculous oil performed various healings on Syrians and Lebanese. Then Merez gave a press conference, in the presence of Metropolitan Jeremiah of France and the representative of the Patriarchate of Antioch in France, Bishop Gabriel.

The wondrous sign continued to be repeated. And not only in Merez's chapel but also elsewhere, when Assaf prayed or participated in the Divine Liturgy or simply mentioned the name of Jesus and the Panagia. On September 17, 1988, during the Divine Liturgy in the Greek church of Saint Stephen on Rue Georges Bizet, the oil gushed for an hour, and all the faithful witnessed it.

The thirty-year-old Assaf was very simple, and with a pure heart. He lived with great humility and simplicity and said that every time the miracle occurred, he was filled with unspeakable joy. He believed that this blessing from God belongs to everyone.

Subsequently, science undertook to investigate the truth of the miracle. A committee was appointed, whose members observed the phenomenon three times, during which they collected the secreted oil and subjected it to biochemical analyses. These examinations were carried out at the Lipid Biochemistry Laboratory of the Pitié-Salpêtrière Hospital in Paris, by Professor J.L. de Gennes. The committee's findings were presented to the public by Metropolitan Jeremiah. According to this, the liquid exhibited the characteristic composition of a vegetable oil.

It contains lipid elements, particularly phytosterols, which are not present in the blood. Furthermore, it is impossible for them to be synthesized by the human body. The liquid also contains cholesterol, a component of animal origin, which is never found in any olive oil. Emphasizing this last point, the committee concluded that under these conditions "the liquid cannot originate from any external supply of olive oil." It also confirmed the undisputed improvement in the health of two individuals who were anointed with the oil secreted from the hands of Bassam Assaf.

And the committee's report concludes as follows: "This event admits no natural or logical explanation. It rather belongs to the multitude of miracles of our Panagia, which the history of the Church has known."

[3]

BIBLIOGRAPHY

1. Athanasiou, Archim., "The Most Holy Theotokos in the life of the monk," journal *Orthodox Witness*, vol. 18, publ. "The Friends of Mount Athos", Nicosia.
2. Andreou Agioreitou, monk, *Gerontikon of Mount Athos*, vol. II, Athens 1980 (2nd ed.).
3. Anonymous, "Unprecedented miracle of the Theotokos to a Syrian Orthodox," journal *Agioreitiki Martyria*, vol. 2, publ. Holy Monastery of Xiropotamou, Mount Athos.
4. Anonymous hesychast, *Niptic Theory*, publ. "Orthodox Kypsele", Thessaloniki 1979.
5. Axiotaki, Andrea, *The Nea Moni of Chios*, Chios 1980 (2nd ed.).
6. Balan Ioanichie, hierom., *Romanian Gerontikon*, publ. "Orthodoxos Kypseli", Thessaloniki 1985.
7. Chatzicharalambous, Char., priest, "The miracle of the Panagia in Orchomenos," journal *Ekklisiastiki Martyria*, vol. 8, Livadia.
8. D.S., Archim., "Magic and... chickpeas," journal *Lychnia Nikopoleos*, vol. 82, publ. Holy Metropolis of Nikopolis, Preveza.
9. Dionysiatou, Theoklitou, monk, *Panagia i Limnia*, publ. Holy Church "The Nativity of the Theotokos", Limni, Euboea 1985.
10. Dramountianos, N., "Narrations," journal *Salpigx Orthodoxias*, vols. 147, 242, and 252. Publ. Holy Metropolis of Florina, Florina.
11. Gkitakou, Michael, *The Monastery of Phaneromeni, Salamis*, Athens 1981 (2nd ed.).
12. Gouvalis, Daniel, Archim., *The Miracle of Faith*, Athens 1985 (3rd ed.).
13. Grigoriatou, Damaskinou, monk, *Journey of the Orthodox Romanian Church*, publ. "Athos", Piraeus.
14. Holy Monastery Eikosifoinissis, *Miracles of Panagia Eikosifoinissis*, Drama 1982.
15. Holy Monastery Panagias Prousiotissis, *Sacred Narration*, Athens 1982.
16. I.M.S., "Gero-Gelasius Simonopetritis," journal *Osios Gregorios*, vol. 13, publ. Holy Monastery of Grigoriou, Mount Athos.
17. Ioannou Moschou, *Leimonarion (Spiritual Meadow)*, trans. Theologou Stavronikitianou, monk, publ. Holy Monastery of Stavronikita, Mount Athos 1983.
18. Iosif, monk, *Elder Joseph the Hesychast*, Mount Athos 1984.
19. Iosif, monk, *Paterikai Morfai Neas Skitis (Pateric Figures of New Skete)*, publ. "To Agion Oros", Thessaloniki 1988.
20. Kaloutsi, Sof., *Akolouthia kai paraklitikos kanon Panagias tis Myrtidiotissis (Service*

and Supplicatory Canon of Panagia Myrtidiotissa), Athens 1981 (3rd ed.).
21. Kapitoglou, N., "Miracles that happen today," journal *Kivotos*, vols. 21 and 22, Athens.
22. Karathanou, Sot., *Of the mountain and the plain*, Athens 1978.
23. Lagourou, Styl., *Miracles of the Megalochari*, vol. I, publ. "Tinos", Athens.
24. Lazarou Dionysiatou, monk, *Dionysiatikai diigiseis (Dionysian Narrations)*, publ. Holy Monastery of Dionysiou, Mount Athos 1989 (2nd ed.).
25. Maximou, hierom., *The Mother of Christians*, Mount Athos 1989.
26. Moiscos, monk, "The history of a copy of the icon "Axion Esti"," journal *Orthodox Witness*, vol. 18, publ. "The Friends of Mount Athos", Nicosia.
27. Nikiforou, presbyter, *Osios Andreas o dia Christon salos (Saint Andrew the Fool-for-Christ)*, trans. Isaac, monk, publ. Holy Monastery Paraklitou, Oropos 1990 (6th ed.).
28. Nikodimou Agioreitou, saint, *Neon Eklogion*, publ. "Astir", Athens 1974.
29. N.R., "1940: The Trumpet Call of the War," journal *Pros tin Nikin*, vol. 16, publ. "O Sotir", Athens.
30. Panagopoulou, D., *Holy Monastery Malevis*, Athens.
31. *Russian Life*, issue 7969/14-5-1974, (Russian newspaper).
32. Savva, "The Panagia in the life of Papa-Tychon," journal *Orthodox Witness*, vol. 18, publ. "The Friends of Mount Athos", Nicosia.
33. Sperantza, Theodosiou, *I Panagia i Chrysopigi tis Sifnou (The Panagia Chrysopigi of Sifnos)*, Athens 1949.
34. Terzaki, Angelou, *Greek Epic 1940-41*, publ. "Estia", Athens 1980 (2nd ed.).
35. Tigka, Th.K., *I eikona tis Megalocharis (The Icon of the Megalochari)*, Athens 1963 (2nd ed.).
36. Timotheou, Archim., *Osios Serafeim tou Sarof (Saint Seraphim of Sarov)*, publ. Holy Monastery Paraklitou, Oropos 1991 (3rd ed.).
37. Tsakou, Ioannou, priest, "A miracle at a camp," journal *Agioreitiki Martyria*, vol. 1, publ. Holy Monastery of Xiropotamou, Mount Athos.
38. Vasileiou, Ant., *The Evangelistria*, Thivai (Thebes) 1968.
39. Vasilopoulou, Charalambous, Archim., *Miracles of the Panagia*, publ. "Orthodoxos Typos", Athens 1973 (2nd ed.).
40. Vasilopoulou, Charalambous, Archim., *The Life of the Panagia*, publ. "Orthodoxos Typos", Athens 1970.
41. Viktoros, Matthaiou monk (ed.), *Great Synaxaristes of the Orthodox Church*, vols. 1-14, Athens 1946-50 (1st ed.).

UNCUT MOUNTAIN PRESS TITLES

Books by Archpriest Peter Heers

Fr. Peter Heers, *The Ecclesiological Renovation of Vatican II: An Orthodox Examination of Rome's Ecumenical Theology Regarding Baptism and the Church*, 2015

Fr. Peter Heers, *The Missionary Origins of Modern Ecumenism: Milestones Leading up to 1920*, 2007

Fr. Peter Heers, *Formation in the Love of Truth*, 2024

The Works of our Father Among the Saints, Nikodemos the Hagiorite

Vol. 1: *Exomologetarion: A Manual of Confession*

Vol. 2: *Concerning Frequent Communion of the Immaculate Mysteries of Christ*

Vol. 3: *Confession of Faith*

The Works of our Father Among the Saints, St. Hilarion (Troitsky)

Vol. 1: *On the Dogma of the Church: An Historical Overview of the Sources of Ecclesiology*

The Works of our Father Among the Saints, St. Raphael of Brooklyn

Vol. 1: *In Defense of St. Cyprian*

Vol. 2: *On the Steadfastness of the Orthodox Church*

Vol. 3: *Union with Rome?*

Other Available Titles

St. Gregory Palamas, *Apodictic Treatises on the Procession of the Holy Spirit*

Elder Cleopa of Romania, *The Truth of our Faith*

Elder Cleopa of Romania, *The Truth of our Faith, Vol. II*

Fr. John Romanides, *Patristic Theology: The University Lectures of Fr. John Romanides*

Demetrios Aslanidis and Monk Damascene Grigoriatis, *Apostle to Zaire: The Life and Legacy of Blessed Father Cosmas of Grigoriou*

Protopresbyter Anastasios Gotsopoulos, *On Common Prayer with the Heterodox According to the Canons of the Church*

Robert Spencer, *The Church and the Pope*

G. M. Davis, *Antichrist: The Fulfillment of Globalization*